THE CONSCIOUS YOU

BREAKING DOWN THE BARRIERS TO CONSCIOUSLY CREATE YOUR BEST LIFE

ALISON CALLAN

Disclaimer

Although the author and publisher have made every effort to ensure that the information in this book was correct at press time, the author and publisher do not assume and hereby disclaim any liability to any party for any loss, damage, or disruption caused by errors or omissions, whether such errors or omissions result from negligence, accident, or any other cause.

ISBN:9781696532969
ISBN13

PRAISE FOR THE CONSCIOUS YOU

The Conscious You - An absolute gem of a book!

A must read for everyone.

The contribution from each of the Authors is exceptional and the information and knowledge they share is thought provoking for anyone who has experienced similar circumstances. I saw myself in more than one of the chapters and it has left me feeling uplifted, that I am not alone in the way I perceive things, and I will certainly be reading it again, more than once. It is one of those books that you hold onto as a "go to" guide for life.

It will become that book I reach for when I need that push in the right direction. My heartfelt congratulations to each and every one of the Authors who shared their stories, your words will help many.

Abigail Horne

Entrepreneur

Wow! What can I say? This book is incredible, I started reading and literally couldn't stop.

So many of us go through the emotions of life and more often than not don't question why. We rationalise with, "It's what everyone does" or "That's life". Sadly, many of us have disconnected from our desires for varying reasons, Alison and her co-authors take you through step by step how you can change these thoughts which in result will enable you to live out your true desires.

The vulnerability and the hurdles these ladies have experienced has filled me with both tears and joy, thank you for sharing with us. I know these experiences and techniques you have shared will enhance many lives.

After reading this book I have set new intentions, conscious choices and reconnected with my why.

I am excited, energised and consciously creating my future.

Now it's your turn readers...

Katie Helliwell

Celebrity Psychic Medium

DEDICATION

To every woman reading this book – we see you, we feel you, we are you. We write from our hearts to yours with the intention of reminding you of your power, purpose and inner wisdom.

You already have within you the power to transform and consciously create your best life. Your Conscious Mind believes in you (*and so do we*), so let's turn up the volume and start consciously creating!

To Samantha, Jude, Beck, Carey, and Leesa – Thank You for sharing your journeys. I know that everyone woman who reads this book will feel the love, care, thought and soul you have put into its making. The gifts you impart in this book are timeless and priceless and I know the energy poured into your words will break down many barriers and enable others to embrace their '*Conscious You*' and create their best lives.

To our ancestors and future generations, this is our gift to you.

With immense love and gratitude,

Alison Callan

WITH CLARITY COMES PURPOSE AND DIRECTION.... THROUGH CONSCIOUS CREATION COMES THE EXPERIENCE

CONTENTS

“

SOMETHING MAGICAL IS HAPPENING TODAY,
SOMETHING
MAGICAL IS COMING MY WAY.

UNLEASH THE CONSCIOUS YOU!

THE CONSCIOUS YOU

BY ALISON CALLAN

'Living a life you love and deserve is an evolution of self, a skill you develop that serves for all time'.

Imagine what it would be like to be living a life that you truly want. I am curious as to what that would look like for you.

Time and time again I hear a lot about what people *don't* want, yet rarely does a conversation begin with hopes, aspirations and dreams. How wonderful would it be to live a little more in this reality, focusing more on what you *do* want?

I whole heartedly believe that it is entirely possible, and perhaps this book is the nudge to get you started in that direction. *The Conscious You* is about the ability to bring something to your awareness in the present moment. Awareness by way of feelings, emotions, triggers or behaviours which activate a desire for change to occur so that we invite more of what we *do* want into our life.

This book is a tool to support you in consciously creating your best life, through connecting you to *The Conscious You* to understand your current subconscious programs, values and beliefs. This book is designed to get you thinking, to self-enquire, and to learn how to consciously create your wants and desires. All whilst uncovering subconscious blocks, patterns and beliefs that are holding you back from living your best life.

Throughout this book you are going to hear stories, be given examples, and asked thought provoking questions to consider, with the intention of optimising your experience of the tools relayed in these pages. With the expectation that you will come back to it, over and over again to further expand and explore. Because once you start learning how to Consciously Create your best life, you won't want to stop, and I am a perfect example!

Let me tell you how I got started.

Consciously Creating my best life wasn't always the plan. For years, I didn't even know what that meant, I had no idea that I wasn't living my best life. I had a tonne of dreams and hopes for the future, with no timeframe, idea or action plan on how to make them a reality. At that point in my life I had no understanding that it was my responsibility to make things happen, to be conscious with the decisions I made, the actions I took, knowing that these decisions were connected and leading me towards my happiness and success. I was without an overall plan, or direction; my big picture thinking was limited to days or weeks ahead.

It wasn't until I consciously chose to become a mum and start a family, that everything shifted within me. My perspective on the life I was living and what would bring me happiness evolved into something that took me quite by surprise.

I was working the regular nine to five on the corporate career ladder, satisfied with my daily contribution, but with no true purpose in my sights. I had emigrated to New Zealand from the UK, which was a dream in itself. I had a fabulous partner, home and lifestyle, and yet I had this deep yearning to do more in the world, outside of the recent motherhood aspirations I was building.

Ever since I was young I had felt there was more to me and my existence, I had never been able to put my finger on what it was other than a feeling that something was around the corner and with each corner I passed there was still only that feeling... nothing ever eventuated.

When I look back to my corporate days, existing in what I call my corporate haze – I realise that I was barely living, rather I was, '*going through the motions*'. I would have moments of feeling satisfied for a short while from small wins at work, there was always this feeling, a knowing, a *need,* to do and be more that never went away completely.

As soon as I became a mum, I awoke to the need within me to take action and be an inspiration to my children and others. To help them awaken to the fact that if they have an underlying lurking feeling of wanting to do and be more in the world, then it's because they are meant to be doing and being more. Now it is time to actively and consciously create the steps to connect *you* to that same calling.

Let me be clear, it wasn't a moment of divine inspiration that set me on this mission and unleashed my purpose. If only it were that easy! No, I went through challenges and a lot of self-doubt before I appreciated and understood what this life was going to mean to me, and how I was going to live it to the best of my capabilities.

Being on the hamster wheel of life, going through the motions, accepting small wins was no longer enough for me. So, I decided to go on a quest of sorts, to connect to my inner truth, and do something about that deep lurking feeling that I was missing something.

Knowing what lit me up and knowing how I could help and support people didn't mean that life would be easier for me. I had to embrace my fears and learn to control them, I had to learn to prioritise myself, I had to connect deeply with others and communicate clearly, and I had to commit to working on myself every single day. Deciding to pursue my dream to do and be more in the world simply meant that I had a direction and a passion to pursue. Deciding that something was important to me, meant I felt connected to something bigger than myself. It felt like I was contributing in a much bigger way and all of a sudden the bigger picture became clear and I knew what my next steps needed to be.

I know I am not alone in this journey, nor do I believe that I am the only one who has kept that secret feeling of knowing they were meant to do and be more in the world. I know that you too have been looking around those corners seeking for understanding and purpose, that elusive something more.

I know because I work with women like you, like me, who have courageously stepped into the place mentally, emotionally and physically where they can expand. Where they can listen to the calling they have felt and slowly and surely, start to follow it.

Everything starts with ourselves, our journey, our dreams, our wants, needs and environment. We can learn a lot about ourselves here and now, exactly where we are. And this is exactly where we begin.

The Conscious You is an invitation for you to actively work on experiencing more fulfilment, joy and connection in your life.

It is my passion and purpose to awaken women from the average, mundane, the life they have settled for and remind them that there is so much more that they are here to do and be. It starts with evaluating where you are now, letting that deep inner calling lead the way towards those long forgotten or dismissed dreams, and then connecting to your conscious choices, actions and opportunities.

I brought this book into existence with the help of some of my most amazing clients who have actively gone on their own exploration of awakening their most conscious selves. An awakening that has allowed them to uncover their purpose, and in the process has allowed them to create their best lives and businesses. As a result, they have some incredible insights to share with you.

Working with these women while they uncover their purpose, passion and key messages consciously has been an absolute privilege, and I cannot wait to introduce you to them and their insights further on in this book.

Throughout this book you will be shown opportunities and ways of becoming awakened to a more consciously created life and be shown how to take ownership of your choices.

Remember, life doesn't happen to you, it happens for you, and as such we need to take charge and begin to make changes in the moments where we can be present and conscious of our wants, needs and desires. Becoming conscious enables you to get to a place where you feel deserving, worthy and ready to actively reach for your dreams and prioritise your happiness.

The benefit I have experienced from engaging *The Conscious You* is that my level of self-awareness has substantially risen, enabling me to know what I want in the world, who I want to be and how I can start to make the necessary changes to make that happen. I have learnt to trust my subconscious, to understand what it tells me and how it triggers my behaviours. Knowing this now allows me to manage my expectations. Becoming conscious is not about your subconscious mind no longer being in control, it is about making sure that your subconscious is in alignment with the desires of *The Conscious You*, and therefore running the systems and programs that *you* truly want! This will be further explained in the book, so you can activate this level of self-awareness too.

I spent so many years sacrificing my happiness for the next promotion or acknowledgement at work, allowing my relationships and mental and emotional health to suffer. I had got stuck in the rut that my worth and value in the world was only as good as my status at work. There was no integration or reality check. I was living to work, with my only real goal being to make it to a more senior title. When I truly explored my need for that accolade I realised it was connected to my view of success, how I appeared to others. I realised then that I didn't want to live a life based on the perceptions of others. What I realised was that my happiness, freedom and relationships were my success.

Everyone has a different version of what brings them happiness and what success feels like, rarely do we bring our conscious awareness to these aspects of ourselves and prioritise them.

Samantha, Beck, Jude, Leesa, Carey and I are going to take you on our unique journeys to embracing our conscious selves, sharing the power, the purpose and impact of what we learnt along the way. We are sharing our insights into how you too can start to become *The Conscious You*, and live a life you have consciously created, love and deserve.

This is your time and opportunity, grasp it with both hands,

Alison Callan

ABOUT ALISON CALLAN

Alison Callan is an International Award Winning Clarity & Success Coach, Mindfulness Consultant, Neuro-linguistic Programming (NLP) Practitioner, Speaker and Co-Author of the #1 best-selling book 'You Are Meant For More'.

Alison's journey as a female entrepreneur was inspired thanks to her first year as a mum, when she was determined not to buy into the hype surrounding the stress of parenting, and instead chose to create a new vision and belief system for herself to help her overcome potential challenges. This led her to embrace her journey to realising her human and spiritual potential to consciously create her reality.

An empathic and heart-led purposeful business coach to aspiring and existing female entrepreneurs and career women, Alison started her coaching business in New Zealand whilst on parental leave in 2016, following her calling to become an Associate Certified Coach (ACC) with the International Coach Federation (ICF). She grasped the opportunity to create a career path that felt authentic to her, that was truly satisfying and empowering, rather than sticking to the safe path she thought she ought to follow.

As an acclaimed *'self-development junkie'*, Alison has combined her Coaching, Mindfulness, NLP, Spiritual and Self Awareness techniques alongside her Business Acumen and ongoing personal development journey, to actively impact and inspire millions of women globally through her coaching, programs, speaking, collaborations, media features and press.

Alison is passionate about helping women make the necessary lifestyle and business changes, to enable them to reclaim their joy and refocus their minds to create an actively conscious awareness. Her mission is to help and champion the introverted, empathic and intuitive women starting in business or taking their professions by storm, to ensure they step up to be seen, and heard.

Alison doesn't believe that her heart or mind were designed to stay still and her passion for travel certainly has her exploring this beautiful world we live with. For now, you can find Alison, as of 2019, happily living in Brisbane Australia with her two boys, husband, dog and cat.

E: alison@alisoncallan.com

W: www.alisoncallan.com

FG: www.facebook.com/groups/ConsciousCreationers/

L: http://bit.ly/MeonLi

Y: http://bit.ly/MeonYT

Work with Alison:

https://AlisonCallanDiscovery.as.me/Discovery

facebook.com/alisoncallan3c

instagram.com/alison.callan

LIFE IS HAPPENING FOR YOU... ESPECIALLY IF YOU'RE CONSCIOUSLY CREATING IT!

CONNECTING TO YOUR CONSCIOUS

BY ALISON CALLAN

'Consciousness is the ultimate in freedom to living life on your terms, you learn from your past and create your future, while being present'.

To know how to rise from the subconscious you to *The Conscious You* requires energy, commitment, practice and purpose. I say that to prepare you to appreciate and fully commit to the upgrade in your life that will be available to you through connecting to *The Conscious You*.

Grab a pen and some paper, and let's connect you to yours now by asking the following questions;

- What does your current life look like, where are you, what do you do, how do you feel, what surrounds you and who are you spending your time with?

- Now, let me ask you, what would you prefer your life to look like? Where would you be, what would you do, how would you feel, what would be around you and who would you be spending your time with?

I often use this exercise myself to determine what might be out of alignment in my life, and I invite you to do the same. Answering these questions, will likely highlight some synergies and disconnects. Some of this will be due to beliefs, blocks and limits that your subconscious mind has created, absorbed or responded to. Now, this is where the magic lies and let me tell you why.

If you had two life lists:

- list 'A' being your current life and;
- list 'B' being the life you desire

I want to help you realise that you can have the life you desire, to provide you with the tools and skills to achieve the life you desire. By the end of this book you will understand that there is nothing stopping you from achieving the life you desire, all it takes is self-belief, prioritising, a willingness and readiness to change and adapt.

I am not suggesting that in this book we can immediately transform your life, however I am suggesting that with a connection to *The Conscious You*, you will start to see where in your world you can change and upgrade your beliefs, priorities, values, triggers to bring you closer than ever before to your desired life. Understanding how your conscious and subconscious mind works is the first step to unlocking your ability to be, do and have more of what you want in the world.

So, let me ask you another set of questions,

- where in your life are you just going through the motions?
- what do you know, feel and believe is holding you back from achieving the life you desire?

It is so important to know where you are in life and where you want to go. It's also very important to become aware of your current state of subconsciousness so that you can begin to understand or become curious about what is keeping you in the now rather than where you want to be. In this book, we can begin to identify your barriers to consciously creating your best life. If you don't have all the answers at this stage, do not worry, you will get there and we have the rest of this book to support and guide you.

Where you are now is only the start of your journey and we will support you in getting to where you want to be.

Let's start getting you clear on your conscious and subconscious states of being.

Knowing the difference between your conscious and subconscious state is the beginning of tapping into your awareness. Simply put, your level of consciousness is a reflection of your level of awareness around all things in any given moment.

Your conscious mind refers to those moments where you are aware of your internal dialogue, your thoughts, experiences, feelings, memories and sensations in the moment. *The Conscious You* is objective; it is your thinking mind and it is said that we are only in this conscious state for up to 5% [1]of our time.

Your subconscious mind is the mental, emotional processor of activities just below the threshold of your consciousness. Think of it like the hard drive of a computer, storing information and running programs. This hard drive contains mostly learned and absorbed behaviour and allows us to function on autopilot while our conscious mind wanders. It is immensely powerful and controls the functions of our body, such as your breathing rate and heart beats. Our subconscious mind is in control of 95% of how we experience and show up in our lives.

When engaged, *The Conscious You* can pick up on thoughts, feelings and behaviours that arise through the subconscious mind which stores all our beliefs, habits, responses and emotions. The same beliefs, habits, responses and emotions that could be stopping you from living the life you want and deserve! The conscious mind, when aware and invested, can reprogram the subconscious to respond to life in our most favourable of ways.

Before we can consciously reprogram our subconscious mind we need to identify those underlying subconscious programs which could be sabotaging you.

Samantha will be sharing more of this magic with you when

she takes you on the journey of Energetic Communication and it is fair to say that grasping this concept will be life changing for you.

The more we practice living in a state of consciousness the more we actively participate in our lives and experience more of what we desire.

Having this knowledge allows you to question where in your life you need to be more in your conscious state because you are feeling disconnected, disengaged or unfulfilled and then do something about it.

Let me share with you my experience of connecting with my conscious, and the impact and change that occurred in my life as a result. As I have already shared, it had not been my intention to connect to my conscious, I didn't even know I was connecting! I did know that I had a distinct moment of awareness, triggered by my emotions, which led me down the path to uncovering and connecting to my consciousness. Moreover, appreciating the power in it!

It was spring in New Zealand in 2012 and I was looking out over the inlet in Paremata through the patio doors watching the sun go down over the hills and the night descend. I was feeling trapped, isolated and confused. I was struggling to process my feelings, because over the previous twelve weeks I had been so excited and present, on that night I wasn't feeling that way.

After the confusion settled and I could focus, I was able to catch my thoughts and make sense of what I was experiencing. It was sadness.

I had finally reached the magical twelve weeks in my pregnancy and started to share my news with people. David and I were expecting our first child and we were so happy. We had been cultivating the vision of our little family complete and happy and had this perfect dream of what life would be like, full of love and possibilities. Yet everyone else's stories were in complete contrast to ours. I had been met with story after story from seasoned parents who were perpetually exhausted, run ragged and disconnected from their partners. Everyone I spoke to was fixated on the fact that I would never sleep again or have time with my husband; some even felt sorry for me that I didn't have any family close by to help, because it was so difficult parenting and raising a child.

Standing quiet in the moment, surveying the night from my home, my safe place, I realised that until I had shared my news I had been living my life through only my lens, until others had started sharing their views and opinions on me, my vision of becoming a mum, how I was going to control my life, my pregnancy, and birth, were all perfectly planned in my mind.

I realised then that the feelings rising in me weren't fully mine, I was buying into everyone else's stories of no sleep, eternal exhaustion and the never-ending challenges of being a parent.

This generalised belief system I had uncovered, that parenting was hard, exhausting and isolating, was infiltrating my thoughts and emotions, confusing my own expectations of parenthood and diminishing my dreams. And I was not going to let that happen, my vision had kept me hopeful, excited and connected until then. I was not letting that go.

That night, in the spring of 2012, pregnant with my first child Max, looking out onto our deck past the inlet and into the hills, I made a promise to myself.

No matter how hard the pregnancy, birth and parenting challenges might be, I would always remember the conscious choice I made to bring our child into the world, and how much love, happiness and intention had gone into creating this life for us all.

This was my *defining moment*, the moment I started to change my whole life, my whole perspective on life, who I was, what I was becoming and the strength I had to make it my reality.

This promise and conscious choice to be a parent, to remember the power within that decision and the emotions it evoked for me every time I recalled it, became my anchor. Anytime I needed to navigate a situation or decision, I consciously consulted my promise to see if I was in or out of alignment with my commitment to enjoy every moment of being a parent and whether this opportunity or decision supported me to uphold that.

This was my first experience of connecting to my purpose, uncovering my '*why*' and choosing to live intentionally to Consciously Create my best life, *our* best life.

This experience was extremely transformative for me. I realised that I was capable of being influenced by others mentally and emotionally. I learnt that I needed to spend time self-enquiring, understanding my thoughts and processing them while I was experiencing them, so that I could choose what was *my* truth.

Little did I know that I had just caught my subconscious creating a new program about parenthood through the uncomfortable feelings and emotions of confusion and sadness that I was experiencing. I had given myself the space and time to check in on what was happening and as a result I consciously changed the program on this belief, communicating with my subconscious what was in fact more important to me, *my own* vision!

Remembering my promise, the anchor I created, kept me centred and mindful during my parental leave with Max. And I can honestly say it was the longest, happiest and healthiest twelve months I have ever experienced.

I truly believe that this experience was possible because I consciously chose not to succumb to the fear of believing that parenting had to be hard. Because I didn't succumb to this belief, because I chose to notice what I was experiencing. My subconscious programming became attached and fixated on my promise, that I was in control, that I had purpose and that connecting to my conscious was of importance.

I allowed the future to unfold naturally, retaining all my power and sense of control through continuing to connect to my consciousness.

Little did I know at that time the power in my discovery and the journey my curiosity would take me on to learn more, do more and become more.

Over time, I continued to identify my subconscious behaviours, consciously catching those thoughts that felt off, confusing, and chose to make my changes consciously.

I want this for you too, and here is how you can start to make the shift to *The Conscious You*;

- Get familiar with your conscious mind, learn to recognise when it is naturally in control.
- Start to notice when your subconscious programs come into play and get curious about what they tell you.
- Write your list 'A' for what your life looks like presently, where are you, what do you do, how do you feel, what surrounds you and who are you spending your time with?
- Write your list 'B' for what you would prefer your life to look like? Where would you be, what would you do, how would you feel, what would be around you and who would you be spending your time with?
- Identify where in your life you're going through the motions.
- Focus on each answer and without too much thinking, allow your subconscious to respond to the questions;

    ◊ *what do you know about what is holding you back?*
    ◊ *what do you feel about what is holding you back?*

◊ *what do you believe about what is holding you back?*

- Notice any disconnects and similarities between all of these responses? What stands out to you?
- Notice where you would like to start on changing your story.

TRUST YOUR UNCONSCIOUS MIND.

Alison Callan

VALUING YOUR BELIEFS AND BELIEVING YOUR VALUES

BY ALISON CALLAN

'Values and beliefs are the story of your soul'

Your values and beliefs are something I want to draw your attention to as they work together so beautifully to support you in your visions. Especially when your visions are aligned with your values and beliefs. This is why we are looking at them now, to determine what visions, values and beliefs are, so that you know how they fit into the evolution of *The Conscious You*.

This is where you start to trust the subconscious mind because its primary role is to keep you safe. And our subconscious programming has been created to do just that. And now that you know more about the benefits of connecting to *The Conscious You*, you can do and be even better, if you choose to.

You will have lots of values and beliefs for a multitude of things in your life, from relationships, to work or business and beyond. Your set of values and beliefs about certain aspects of your life will need to be known and understood before you can attempt to make any changes to *The Conscious You,* and here is why.

If *The Conscious You* is only present for 5% of the time, then your values and beliefs are running the other 95% of the time as your subconscious programs. What exactly are they, and what do they have to do with consciously creating your best life?

Well, what if I were to explain it like this. Your values are a code by which you have chosen to live your life. Your values determine the importance of things, actions or behaviours which you live your life by. In a narrow sense your values are a moral compass of sorts which, to you, denote what is good, worthwhile or desirable in your world. These values drive your behaviours and they steer you towards or away from decisions, situations or behaviours.

Your belief is your truth, which is entirely unique to you based on your personal attitude, concepts and experiences. Beliefs are contextual and individual to each of us as they arise from our learned behaviours and experiences. These beliefs become your anchors to guide you through your life.

It's important to understand that we have values and beliefs that are created and stored over time as our subconscious programs to support us to better navigate this world. Those values and beliefs being challenged are of equal importance, because we also store programs around how we respond and behave should we come into contact with our opposites.

So, how do your values and beliefs work together and how do they impact and influence *The Conscious You?*

Here is a black and white example of a value and belief system working;

If you had a value of honesty, and your belief was that honesty is imperative in all relationships in order to trust. Then should you be faced with a situation where someone kept something from you, you might find that immediately you experience feelings of distrust, because subconsciously in your world your values and beliefs are very simple. However, if the something that were being kept from you were a surprise party, so the intention had been good, it might still cause you some internal conflict unknowingly which you feel because of the value and belief system you hold and what it represents to you. Being aware of these will enable *The Conscious You* to be involved and engaged with your subconscious programming on a conscious level. Being conscious of this will allow you to determine where these values and beliefs may be misaligned and need a little more context and an upgrade.

If you have come across any of my work previously then you will know that I hold beliefs in very high regard. Whereas a lot of people prefer to work on their mindset first, I know that you cannot tell yourself affirmations daily expecting them to work, if they are in direct conflict with or misaligned with your subconscious beliefs.

For example, if I want to start a new routine like joining a gym, I couldn't just tell myself daily that I love going to the gym to give me the motivation to consistently go and embed this as a new routine. I would need there to be an underlying belief that gyms were beneficial and useful to me, and that I believed in that method of getting fit in order to stabilise and truly commit to going. If my underlying belief was that gyms are only a fad, then it's more likely that I will struggle with my ongoing commitment because my belief and mindset are misaligned and not communicating the same message.

Becoming aware of your values and beliefs enables you to optimise your re-programming of your subconscious mind, to support all the subconscious patterns and behaviours to be in alignment with your values and beliefs which form your key drivers to do or not do things in your world.

Going back to my story I found a lot of insights in exploring and uncovering my values and beliefs in many aspects of my world. The more I travelled outside of the parameters of what I knew, of what felt comfortable in varying situations, the more insight I had of myself. As my self-awareness increased through this introspection, it also meant that my subconscious programs were tested a lot!

Becoming conscious in my pursuit of my best life, to create my reality and accept full responsibility for it has transformed me, and it is my intention to show you that this is possible for you too.

Firstly though, let me tell you about an experience where my beliefs and values were tested, and so was I.

I was at a crossroads in my life in 2017. I was working full time in corporate, the long and short of it was that I had hit many personal limits of my beliefs in business and wasn't doing the necessary personal work to move through them. So, I took an easy option, asked the Universe to provide me with a dream job that would also support my business to grow. Sure enough, the Universe had my back and the job came to pass, though after a while I was shown why I was not meant to go backwards! The environment and culture drained me, it wasn't somewhere I could thrive, and it began to make me unwell. I wanted to leave but I had to find *'the right time'*. I knew being at work surrounded by a place and people I couldn't align with, made me a shadow of myself. Being in that environment, the self-doubt, lack of confidence and ability to promote myself took an imploding nose dive. I checked out mentally, physically and emotionally.

My spirit was crushed, confined and I couldn't escape. I was waiting for the '*right time*' to leave, '*when my business was a little more established*', when I felt a '*little better*'. Until then I was going through the motions. Sound familiar?! I was on that hamster wheel again, though this time I should have known better! I was so unhappy and unwell, and as a result my family was now suffering. I had promised myself that my needs were important, that being happy and successful in my own right, that reaching my potential and having a goal was in fact in my family's best interests as they'd get the best of me. Yet, I was missing something....

Clarity hit, I had never made a promise to myself when I created my business, there had never been any intention or conscious choice. I just started the business to get my Coaching accreditation. I realised that I had never taken myself seriously or appreciated all I had accomplished. I played it safe and small. Without my promise and overriding reminder of my purpose and drive within my business, there was nothing to fall back on. Nothing to remind me of my '*Why*', to anchor me to my greater purpose and centre me when I was doubting my abilities.

It finally clicked one day when I was sitting at my desk, in what I had started to call the '*soul destroying day job*'. I recalled my promise to myself about enjoying the moments with my boys, making the most of every hour regardless of how easy or challenging. It struck me, I wasn't afraid of hard work, I never had been. I was tired of *meaningless* work and I was tired of not being present for my boys. The misery I was feeling, of being stuck in a job that didn't align with my values or beliefs, was filtering into every aspect of my life, business and relationships. Staying confined was slowly killing my spirit and I was losing myself, which meant I was losing everything.

I was so annoyed at myself because with this realisation was another one. This was all on me. Consciously noticing this, and what I had chosen, was in direct conflict with my promise to myself as a mother – no matter how hard parenting got I would enjoy it. Well, parenting means showing your children what's acceptable and what isn't. If I wasn't willing to put my happiness above all else, what was I teaching them?

Enough was enough, I chose Me! With *The Conscious You* back in control I consciously chose to quit the day job, immediately.

The relief I felt, the weight that dissipated immediately, the exhilaration at realising that my life was meant to be enjoyed, that my values and beliefs needed to be acknowledged and honoured. How on earth had I forgotten that? Especially after all I had already experienced! The fact that I could tell my boys that I was walking my talk consistently, was so heart-warming. I could be the best version of myself for me, for my boys and for my husband, who inspire me to want success within my own right, to want to reach my potential every single day.

I made a promise there and then, that I would never go for the '*easy out*' option again. I couldn't. Through *The Conscious You*, I chose to uphold my values and beliefs as anchors where I still held them to be true, and I learnt to recognise the trigger of incongruence with my values and beliefs and the external world. I learnt a lot about myself going through that pattern for a second time.

There are many insights that I have learnt and implemented into my daily life through connecting to my *Conscious You*. These have become values and beliefs that guide me in all areas of my life to strive to be a better me, and I would like to share them with you. With the intention that they might be a guiding light in the darkness to trigger your own beliefs and values, or to find more insights of your own.

Test the following perceptions, values and beliefs out for yourself. Explore their meaning for you, and give the practices a go, keep what connects with you, and see what else might also come up for you as a result. Most importantly have fun with it!

'Never allow your assumptions of how a situation might unfold to rule your experiences and expectations'.

We are naturally and subconsciously wired to be processing situations all of the time, based on what we have already experienced. Our brain is trying to categorise and easily allow us to act and respond according to our past similar experiences. This is wonderful in some situations where we can manage on autopilot, yet there are a lot of opportunities missed to truly rewrite a story, if only we were engaging *The Conscious You.*

Now this also expands to inner stories, namely when we are planning ahead for an eventuality our subconscious often leads us down a repetitive scenario where we might begin to attach assumptions and judgements to an unlived experience which also enables emotions to rise and be categorised into these events.

The Conscious You allows consideration, a pause for awareness where categories of judgements or assumptions may not be needed, and therefore where emotions can be managed.

If you notice yourself entering a situation with a pre-planned assumption for a reaction or outcome, you are allowing your belief in yourself to be questioned, should it not go the way you expected.

One of two things might occur; you sabotage the outcome or response to prove your initial assumption correct, as we all love to be right, or you start to undermine and question yourself and your abilities.

To re-write this for yourself and become *The Conscious You*;

- Begin to identify when you create assumptions, and consider how you would approach the situation differently if they were removed?
- Imagine a situation where this practice would have been of support to you.
- How can you recall it in future instances where it may be of support?

'When you consciously create your 'Why', you have purpose and intention'

Your '*Why*' is the internal compass that is designed to keep you in alignment when you need it the most. Everything you do, that is connected to that space, has meaning and feeling and is associated heavily with your values. This is how I confidently make all of my life and business decisions by keeping connected to this meaning and purpose that I have consciously created. My '*Why*' has evolved over time and has become my anchor in many challenging situations.

The Conscious You remembers this '*Why*' and keeps your internal compass involved and connected to all opportunities, challenges and decisions. Knowing what it is that drives you, gets you doing all that you do, and enables you to feel fulfilled is the very definition of your '*Why*'. Defining it for yourself and creating conscious laser like focus on it, can be immensely powerful in being present.

Here are some questions to ask yourself to help you in getting consciously connected to a more *Conscious You*;

- What is your '*Why*', personally and professionally? Are they aligned?
- What are the emotions connected to your '*Why*' ? How does it make you feel?
- Consider how knowing your '*Why*' will support you to successfully navigate all obstacles in your life.
- What can you do to remind yourself to recall and tap into your '*Why*' regularly?

'Your experiences can spark a passion that can be used to teach others and light a pathway to your purpose'.

Everyone is searching for a purpose, and we each have a distinct part to play in our life journey. The subconscious you keeps you actively in a comfortable cycle of life, with what it knows and can easily and comfortably control. *The Conscious You* is often picking up on something more that is lurking and wanting to be explored, maybe a forgotten dream or experience. Carey shares with you later about *Consciously Restarting* in life, and the importance of a connection to her purpose in her experience of starting over.

Our subconscious keeps us limited in our thinking and being, based on our past experiences. Whereas our conscious allows us to be infinite and expansive when present, as we learn that our past experiences allow us to improve and develop.

It doesn't matter the story that someone else has told, a similar experience that may have been shared numerous times. *Your* story, perspective and insights matter and they need to be heard. Each of us will connect with an experience differently with different people at different times. It is our unique expression of our experiences that needs to be brought to light and shared with the world.

I believe we have had these experiences for a reason, our individual interpretations and voice matter and will reach those they are meant to. We just have to find the defining moment, the experience and truly acknowledge it's meaning within our lives to find its value for others, and ourselves.

To begin to find your *Conscious You's* purpose and meaning in life so far, you can task yourself with these exercises;

- Make a list of your life experiences, note how you feel about them, how you journeyed through them and which ones you are most proud of.
- Journal the story and identify what you can teach others from your experience.
- Connect this to your '*Why*' insights, and you will begin to uncover your present purpose.

* * *

> ***'Don't waste time and energy on an imagined future, especially if it makes you feel powerless and out of control'.***

There are honestly so many imagined states of being we might one day experience. However, if we spend any of our present moments thinking about them, we start to actively feel what we would if we were already there.

Our emotions are so powerful that when we spend time needlessly worrying, we are emotionally starting to live out that imagined existence, which is when the worry and fear take over, and we begin to feel powerless and out of control. We start to believe that our future is determined, and we are doomed for that existence, when in fact that is not the case.

You must appreciate that we are created and taught to be mindful of risks and hazards, and naturally it's in our own best interests to protect ourselves. Sometimes these experiences can be counterproductive though, because our subconscious gets carried away allowing our fears and doubts to be rampant.

The Conscious You when engaged, can identify this subconscious behaviour and pull you back into the present, attaching a more pleasing expectation, outcome and emotions to the scenario you're scoping out. This is a far better use of your energy, and *Samantha's* chapter will explain a lot more on this in respect to *Energetic Communication.*

To activate your more conscious mind in these situations, be sure to;

- Be self-aware.
- Be mindful of the time, energy and focus you give to thoughts which lead you astray and make you feel powerless and out of control. Therefore, identify those emotions and triggers.
- Instead stay in the moment and find your peace there.
- Concentrate on feeling more successful, assertive, and confident when you consider your future.

Allowing yourself to trust that you are consciously creating your most empowered and connected version of your future in alignment with your '*Why*', knowing that all your assumptions and judgements are not needed, makes for a pretty powerful and *Conscious You.*

'Get Perspective'.

As incredible as it is to create a life and be able to share it, there is also the flip side that we can lose a life. When I was pregnant with my second son, Liam, my Mum had some health issues and was eventually diagnosed with cancer. I was distraught and faced with the very real possibility that a change of this magnitude in my life could occur at any moment. The thought of losing my mum was deeply shocking, we are so close and connected but there was nothing I could do to take the pain away. My mum has always been an exemplary role model, so she went on about her day with a sensational attitude to be in the moment and to focus on the joys, knowing she was in control of her dis-ease. And to this day, she is still in control!

This experience brought me perspective, and reminded me to maximise the time that I have and appreciate that every single day should be regarded as a gift. A privilege to be a part of, an honour to create your existence and a right to impact and influence the world for the greater good. I wasn't going to waste a moment! I was going to be very aware of my emotions and make conscious choices, to create my day, ensuring I never lost perspective.

It also reminded me how important my role was as a mother and role model, a gift in itself.

Here are some ways that you can ensure your connection to your perspective, incorporating some of the other insights into *The Conscious You*:

- Connect to what brings you perspective.
- Where would perspective be most useful for you in your life right now?
- Create a morning mindset ritual to consciously connect to your '*Why*', your vision for your future, so you begin your day with the perspective that is going to ensure you make the most of it and attribute your actions and responses to life through this lens. So that you consciously bring your best self to your day, every day.

Gaining perspective like this allows us to remember our place in the world, to be a part of something bigger, greater and to be grateful for the experiences, always looking for the meaning.

'When stuck in the unknown, request that the Universe provide an answer, then listen'.

This insight has always been my go-to remedy for confusion and indecision, and a powerful one at that. Even engaging and developing your connection to *The Conscious You*, there are still instances where you do not know what to do, think or feel. Sometimes we need to let go in a situation and ask for support and be open to it when it comes. Please know that everything happens for you, not to you and as such you have the power to ask for help and guidance. The secret to being able to receive the answer is in your ability to let go of any specifically desired outcome that you may want. Detaching from your own expectations and trusting that you'll be shown the answer and be able to recognise it when delivered is key. I have used this practise many times, and often the answer hasn't been what I wanted, expected or been easy. It has always been what I needed, and I believe that you too can consciously request for universal support and guidance.

When you need to offer up a situation for universal support ensure that you do so from a conscious space, so that you are actively open to receiving the response when it is presented. Here is how you can ask for this guidance for yourself:

- Ask a specific question before your dream state or during meditation.
- Once you have been clear in your question, make it specific then intentionally let the desire for an answer go.

- Let go of your preference to have a particular answer delivered. Be open to the options, they may pleasantly surprise you.
- Imagine detaching from the need for an outcome, knowing that it's already on its way.
- Consciously continue in your days with the resolution that an answer will be presented in the perfect time.
- Be patient!

Remember that sometimes we only see the answers to our questions in reflection, not everything can be seen, experienced and appreciated during the occurrence. There is a reason that hindsight is universally known as a wonderful gift!

This next insight is probably one of the biggest and most critical learnings of my existence, one I am so grateful to have learnt and been able to absorb.

> ***'It is more important what I think of myself, than what others think of me!'***

I have always been my own worst critic; I was always projecting my fears through other's eyes. Telling myself stories of what others must think of me, or how they must be interpreting my actions. This thinking kept me small and timid for far too long. I would tell myself that it did not matter what others said or did, but it was a wasted effort because I didn't believe it!

It wasn't until I realised that I was the most important person in my life, and that ultimately I needed to turn my attention and focus on what I thought of myself and how I perceived myself and whether my actions and words were true and in alignment with my values, did I finally grasp this insight!

I could finally see that if I was worried about what other people were thinking, then I was already considering that perspective subconsciously for myself. Otherwise those thoughts would not have even occurred to me. So, I learnt to see my worries of what others may think of me as my guidance system to check in on what I subconsciously thought and stopped projecting my internal struggles and dialogue onto others, and instead learnt to understand and manage it consciously.

Wouldn't it feel so much more powerful a connection to have with yourself if you understood what it was you thought of yourself, what you liked and even loved about yourself, and what you wanted to work on?

Well, here is the practise that you can use to tap into this insight;

- Notice when you are contemplating an outcome based on your assumptions of other people's perceptions.
- Enquire with yourself as to whether this is actually your internal fear, worry or belief.
- Remember that what you think of yourself is of critical importance and that this inner work always needs addressing.
- Turn your compassion inwards, be kind and curious

towards your responses without attaching other people to your journey.

So far you have been asked a lot of questions to get you connecting to your thinking mind, *The Conscious You*. It is not until you are asked questions such as these that you start to actively open yourself up to the possibilities of your potential.

With my own journey and every person that I have had the pleasure of working with, our connection to our consciousness was created through an experience, which started each of us on a journey of purpose and meaning, to firstly better understand ourselves, in order to understand others.

This isn't to say that you must go through an ordeal or a big life event to awaken *The Conscious You*, not at all. There may simply be a moment that you will recall that begins your unique personal process. For each of us, it wasn't the events that we experienced, good or challenging, it was our response to them in a moment that changed us because we noticed the full experience.

The following chapters will connect you to more insights, beliefs, stories and experiences through our revelations on embracing *The Conscious You* in the areas of, communication, connection, restarting your life, breaking down the barriers to stagnant spaces and anxious episodes. We have consciously and intentionally shared aspects of our journeys to inspire, build curiosity and support you in your connection to *The Conscious You*.

Take notes on what stands out to you and start to work on one aspect of *The Conscious You* at a time. There is no need to rush or incorporate more than one insight or change at a time, as each one will take time to rise from your subconscious to understand the program and belief. For you to consciously choose to accept it, change it or delete it. This then takes time and practice to naturally evolve from a conscious aspect to a new and improved subconscious one of your choosing.

For now, take a note of where in your life you most want to be connected to *The Conscious You*. By merely letting yourself be aware of your desire to change from where you are now, to where you desire to be, you will start to experience and notice what comes up through your subconscious to be explored. The intention alone sets a powerful change in motion, so let's see what you start to uncover and where in your life you can begin to Consciously Create.

EVERY ACTION HAS AN INTENTION, CONSCIOUSLY OR UNCONSCIOUSLY — WOULDN'T IT BE MAGICAL TO KNOW IT'S PURPOSE AND CHOOSE TO EMBRACE, DELETE OR REPROGRAM IT?

— Alison Callan —

YOU ARE NOT YOUR EMOTIONS

BY ALISON CALLAN

'Everything is neutral until you attach either a positive or negative emotion to it'

Emotions can tell us so much, consciously and unconsciously as they are experienced and created through our subconscious programming. They can be attached to events, words, songs, movements, there are no limits to how emotions rise within us.

One thing I can be very confident in stating to you, is that you are not your emotions.

Oftentimes I hear people referring to themselves as an emotion, for example stressed, anxious or angry. These are emotions we experience, and they are not infinite. Yes, they leave us with feelings which last longer. Make no mistake, we are in control of what we experience, yes, even down to our emotions.

These labels do not define us. You are not stressed, you're experiencing stress. You are not anxious, you are experiencing anxiety, it is a physical manifestation of an emotion that you experience very really in your body. I appreciate the depth of the emotions we experience, and I do not intend to diminish them in any way, they can be life changing or limiting, however they are still an experience.

Why are emotions even being touched on, I hear you ask. Well, that's a great question and I have a simple answer for you. Because emotions can be great triggers for *The Conscious You* to kick into play, for that glorious 5% of your day!

If you can identify your emotions readily you will start to be present and conscious of the ones you enjoy experiencing more, as well as the ones that you do not want to be experiencing.

Now, if you were to notice the ones that you do not want to experience first, because they are usually the ones that grab your attention immediately, then you can follow that emotion back to a source, a trigger that created that state. When you identify that trigger, you can become aware of the subconscious program that started the chain of events into motion. Then you can consciously choose to keep that program in your subconscious or you can consciously choose to create a newer, updated program, and elicit a new and improved emotion and response when similar situations may occur in the future.

Sounds simple? It is when you know what you are doing, can

identify and control your emotions and learn to detach long enough from a situation to observe and reset! With each attempt you will improve, for now the critical point is to start noticing and actively and consciously identifying your emotions.

Learn to be aware of what's going on inside and outside of you when you experience all your different emotional states.

Learning to manage your emotions and become more emotionally intelligent enables you to have a more fulfilling connected life. When you become aware of your emotions, you begin to appreciate and accept that they all have a purpose for you, and that your subconscious is merely raising a program which is designed to protect you, to raise your awareness or bring something to your attention. Beck will take you on her journey later and further explain how all emotions are valid, and how you can put emotional intelligence into use for the benefit of your connections as well.

To begin to change your states when you notice them rising in situations and they do not support you, you can begin to change them. Firstly, allow *The Conscious You* to be grateful for the response and feeling that arose subconsciously, acknowledge it. Then allow yourself to choose another more preferred state of being and feeling that serves you better and follow through with embodying that emotion fully, physically and mentally absorbing that emotion to better support you in that instance. This starts to override the previous subconscious program, and in turn starts the process for creating an upgraded program that benefits *The Conscious You* through a series of practices, relearned behaviours and conscious choices. It isn't immediate, yet with each opportunity to practise it will become easier to notice, acknowledge and begin to choose your preferred state, remembering that with each time you have a conscious choice. Let's look at an example.

What does success mean to you? Material possessions, an abundant lifestyle, a fantastic relationship, a thriving business, an incredible reputation, or all the above?

To each of us it *is* different. The Dictionary says that success is in fact the achieving of an aim or goal which leads you towards fortune or fame. I would like to reframe that now with you, because success is in fact a feeling. It is an experience that we have.

So my question to you really is, what does success feel like to you?

Now imagine feeling successful, maybe there was time recently where you had cause to celebrate an achievement, a milestone, a win in life or business. Wouldn't it be wonderful if you could bottle that feeling and recreate it every single day?

It is possible, because if you have ever felt success then that experience, when actively recalled, can evoke the same emotions over and over again. Which means you have the ability to make yourself feel successful whenever you want!

So let's get started, I want you to recall a time, and event in your life that's past where you felt successful. Lean into that memory. Take a moment to remember how you physically responded, what your mind was thinking, what you were seeing and hearing, what you were feeling emotionally, allow yourself to feel that success. Allow yourself to fully respond accordingly to that experience, let yourself smile, relax your shoulders, remind yourself of your success. You experienced it once, you can experience it again, as you are now, aren't you?

When you're ready and you have fully embraced that experience, notice what you're feeling. I am sure you're feeling a touch more successful now, you know the feeling of more confidence, that's right, a little more important and even deserving of more success, aren't you?

Now let me ask you;

- Do you remember the first thought you had this morning?
- Do you remember what emotion you felt when you first woke up this morning?
- Have you taken any time today to specifically set an intention for your day, to welcome in success, or seek it out, or any other desired state that you want?

I hear all too often people who get up in the mornings, feeling exhausted, dreading the day beginning because they don't feel ready for their day. This becomes a repeat cycle in their lives. And what's worse is they just get used to it. This is where you might find that you are noticing that this could be a place where you merely go through the motions in your life, and here at the outset of our day is where most people do.

I know how this feels, I can relate to it, can you? Every morning

I used to get sucked into my presumed expectations of the day, without taking notice. Without taking control. This is another example of where I didn't even notice that I wasn't feeling happiness, I was just going through the motions, you will have heard the expression '*living for the weekend*' or '*holiday season syndrome*'.

Well this was before I began to notice and tune into my consciousness, my wants, my needs and change my expectations of my day for the better, and you can do this too. You are not your emotions, but you do control them, so let's start the day in a more successful way, and let's see what shifts.

I am going to share with you my top three ways to turn around your mediocre mornings and consciously create a successful start to your day. So that you can show up in life as the success you already are, with the capacity to bring your best self into every situation. To connect more to the states that you desire, to become more emotionally intelligent and to tap into the subconscious beliefs and programs stopping or supporting you achieving this state, through *The Conscious You*.

One of the tools I am most proud to have brought into existence is the Mindset Pathway, you can find out more about this in chapter 10, for now here is a taster. I created the Mindset Pathway, a tool to actively engage your brain in the feelings, focus areas and attributes you want to bring into your day. Which creates your success mindset.

Like I asked at the beginning here, often at times we don't even notice what our mornings are activated by, so let's take control of our day from the outset and bring our thinking minds, *The Conscious You* to begin by focusing on feeling success.

Here are my three tips for starting your morning the right way to invoke success;

Create a Morning Ritual

Starting your day intentionally to retrain your brain to actively connect to higher vibrational feelings, such as gratitude, success and joy is your first step.

Creating consistency in a morning ritual leads to a better more engaged life and elevated mindset! It is important to notice where any incongruence arises for you in your feelings, because that is a trigger to follow your subconscious patterns to uncover your beliefs about success, or whatever the chosen feeling you desire might be. Remember, your beliefs are more powerful than mindset, to know there needs to be alignment between the two.

Each morning when you wake up you need to allow yourself to tap into your feeling of success. Sit in that for a minute or two and really receive that feeling. This creates a conscious connection to starting your day on top of the world.

For example, my way of tapping into my success feeling is remembering winning a woman in business award in the UK. It wasn't always that, it's evolved over time and so will yours.

So, start with something that has you highly connected to where you felt overwhelming success, gratitude and accomplishment. Remind yourself how awesome you are!

Remember your '*Why*'

Tapping into your '*why*' breeds determination and focus!

You know why you chose to live the lifestyle you have now, what drove you to start your business or career, and more importantly what keeps you in it. How often do you connect to it?

It is now time to own it. Your '*why*' needs to be bigger than its benefits to just you, so stretch yourself to connect to this.

For example, my why is to change all the lives I touch through the message that we can consciously create our most epic life, career and business through conscious connection.

It wasn't always this broad, yet as my business and message has expanded, I have been able to connect to this and it drives me. Your '*why*' needs to drive you too!

Consistency and Accountability are internal jobs!

The more you actively take ownership of wanting this change, and doing all the things required to make it non-negotiable in your routine, the better the overflow of results.

Imagine what it would be like to start everyday with the feeling of success, knowing we are connected to something bigger than ourselves?

I'm curious to know how capable you would feel to start your day and connect with the people in your life in a different way. Bringing forth a success mindset, brings more than just success for you, it has a knock on affect to those around you too.

So, what will it take for you to action this and make your success ritual a habit? Perhaps you could create these boundaries, rules or triggers;

- Setting your alarm, maybe to the Rocky theme tune instead of a normal ring.
- Having a note by your bed to read when you wake.
- Telling your partner what you need to do, to get them to give you encouragement.
- Remembering this commitment before you go to sleep, look forward to waking up and giving it a go.
- Not allowing yourself to have your morning beverage of choice until you've completed this, give yourself a rewards system.

All of this is positive and invoking more of the emotions that we do want in our lives, signals to the subconscious that we have great and purposeful state management, as well as learning to identify and connect to our emotions and use the triggers to our advantage. The fact remains that unless you can connect to the need or the driver that you have for this in your life and know and believe that you deserve to experience success every day and that feeling is already accessible within you, then you will not maintain this momentum or create consistency.

Only you can take responsibility for this. I encourage you to connect to that need for success and how feeling successful will improve multiple areas of your life, relationships, self-confidence, career or business, it's not just about the material!

Explore your emotions, learn to understand and acknowledge

them. Use them in your world to create a better understanding of yourself, knowing you are not labelled by them. They are experiences that you own, can develop and use to connect to *The Conscious You* in order to create a more fulfilling, connected and meaningful life that you love!

“

WITH PURE INTENTION AND HEART, YOUR IMPACT AND INFLUENCE IS GREAT. YOU DO NOT NEED TO HEAR OR KNOW OF THE OUTCOMES TO TRUST IN YOUR POWER AND PURPOSE.

CONSCIOUS INTRODUCTIONS, MEET THE CO-AUTHORS

BY ALISON CALLAN

'Investing in yourself is the very best investment you can ever make'.

You have already read a little of my story, my names Alison. I'm a mum to two boys, a wife, a daughter, friend and Coach. I am a creative, a Speaker, a mindfulness consultant and there is nothing I like more than a deep and meaningful conversation. I found my passion in coaching years before I actively pursued it as a business. Now, I work with incredibly inspiring women all over the world to support them to love life and business. To build, grow and expand in all aspects of their life, business and career with intention. I help them to get clarity to consciously create their best lives and embrace success.

I have the absolute pleasure of introducing you now to some of my most inspirational clients and friends.

Together we brought this book into being because of the passion and purpose we share in committing to our personal and professional development, and the need that we have collectively to share all we know for the good of the world – authentically, honestly and purposefully.

I worked with Samantha initially in The Accelerator MasterCircle program, and then as a 1:1 client. I have seen her commit to developing, growing and co-creating energetically her own personal upgrades and the impact this has had on others and on her business as a result. I can only describe Samantha as a ball full of creative fun, with the essence of magic and miracles and a certain undeniable sass on the side! You'll see what I mean when she shares with you her zone of genius in Conscious and Energetic Communication. This will take your understanding of the conscious and subconscious to the next level!

Beck, was an integral part of The Accelerator MasterCircle program and she established her business and never looked back. Her passion, fun and knowledge astound me every time she talks about connection, it's to be expected that her zone of genius is Conscious Connections. Grab a pen and paper for this one and prepare to be astounded.

Jude has moved mountains in her arena personally and professionally, she has the biggest heart and is a grounded angel for sure. Jude's been working with me in The Conscious Creation Business Accelerator as well as The Accelerator MasterCircle program and I have seen her grow, expand and shed her limits. Experience her chapter to discover how you too can consciously connect to your surroundings.

The transformation in Leesa during her time in The Accelerator MasterCircle has been miraculous. I admit I was sceptical that our spiritual approach, or '*woo-woo*' as she called it, would push her over the edge. Instead she embraced *The Conscious You* and is stepping up to be seen and heard with courage. You simply have to hear her story to appreciate it!

Standing strong and thriving, knowing herself better than ever is Carey. There is no one better I could connect you with to learn how to consciously start over. Carey's kindness, compassion and determination have seen her rebuild a life she is proud of, through connecting to *The Conscious You*.

I am so proud of each and every one of you.

I remember the process that I went through writing my contribution for '*You Are Meant For More*'. I think it was one of the most emotional and expanding processes in personal growth and reflection that I have ever experienced. Having that book, with my story in it, reach number one in multiple categories on launch day was one of the most exhilarating experiences. I knew that I had to bring this experience as an opportunity to my clients when I developed The Accelerator MasterCircle program. After all, this program was to be the most expansive bridge between personal, professional and spiritual development ever, and I knew first-hand the power in sharing your story.

I want you to know that I didn't ask just anyone in my programs or network to contribute to this book. I wanted those who I knew would provide the level of value and knowledge in leadership in their individual zones, exceptionally. Women who were leading the way to positively impacting and influencing in connected relationships, empowered environments, energetic communication, facing anxiety and in restarting life.

I chose these women because I believe in their power, their message and their ability to change the world for the better. And after you read their chapters, I am sure you will too.

The beautiful thing about each of these chapters is that they focus on areas that are dealing with everyday aspects of life. While consistently supporting you to develop and build on your connection to *The Conscious You.*

Now that you know the foundational aspects in connecting to *The Conscious You*, this is where you can start to actively exert its power and see the potential.

“

YOU ARE THE MASTER OF YOUR OWN ENERGY, NOT THE ENERGY OF OTHERS, WITHOUT YOUR DIRECT PERMISSION NOTHING CAN INFLUENCE YOU, YOUR CURRENT STATE OR YOUR FUTURE.

YOU EXCLUSIVELY RULE YOUR WORLD

CONSCIOUS AND ENERGETIC COMMUNICATION

BY SAMANTHA HADDAD

'There is not a human being alive or dead who has not come to earth without a purpose or a legacy to fulfil'.

How often have you felt like you were walking through life numb, aimless without a clue as to why you're even here? Like *The Conscious You* is some distant figure you've never really met before? How often have you asked the questions; '*who am I?*' '*What is the point of my existence?*'

Or my favourite, '*why does this keep happening to me?*'

If you've ever asked yourself these questions, welcome to the club. We all ask these, or similar questions in one form or another, me included.

As Alison shared with you in her story, we all walk through life with this subconscious *'knowing'*, a feeling that we were brought here to do something more, like there is a greater purpose for our existence. Over time, what I have noticed, is that we are told in various ways that we need to get in line, stay in place and be on our best behaviour.

Over the years, we are given strict instructions on how to be, how to act and what to say and do. *"Don't dream big"*, *"stay in your lane"*, *"stick to the rules"*, *"don't rock the boat"*.

Not because those before us are intentionally trying to be cruel, small minded or mean. Our family, our ancestors and our family lineage, as a general rule, expects to dictate how our life unfolds because that is the way we have been taught to believe.

We have been taught that our current reality is a reflection of our internal reality, our thoughts, beliefs, habits and behaviours.

And our internal reality is nurtured by our family who in turn, had their internal reality nurtured by their ancestors, and the pattern continues.

Therefore, if we were to follow the pattern here, if your family has had a poverty mindset and belief for the last fifty to one hundred years; I can almost guarantee that you too hold a poverty mindset and belief and struggle with abundance, wealth and prosperity.

By the same general rule, if your family is athletic, musical, academic or religious it is almost safe to say that you too are naturally connected to these things also.

The impact of this, is that so many of us feel like we aren't living our own life. Like we are doing as we are told, what is expected of us. More often than not, we have largely also become people pleasers. People pleasers who are always struggling with not being perfect, not being enough, and not being worthy just as we are.

Our lives are a repetitive reflection of what our ancestors have been through over and over again. Because part of this pattern that we live is that we constantly seek external gratification. A huge part of our patterning is that we seek external approval, acceptance and praise. That until we reach a certain level of success that our family deems appropriate, we must continue to do all we can to please others, striving for perfection and approval that we are enough.

Our external life is a constant reflection of this internal battle. Part of that internal battle is that we must be more, do more and have more. Because it is what our family wants for us.

How often have you heard parents saying, "*I just want you to have more opportunities than I did, more experiences, more money, more happiness etc.?*"

It is from birth then that we fall into this cycle where we feel this unintended pressure, absorbed from others, that we need to strive for more, but how?

And so, you will notice that we are slowly starting to turn to alternate methods of achieving this preconceived level of success that our family has unintentionally laid out for us. We are turning to alternate methods because the tools and skills that the generations before us have given us are old, out-dated and don't work. Clearly, or our parents or grandparents would have already achieved this preordained level of success we are taught to seek.

So, what you see here is a lifelong pattern that we then pass on to our own children, if we choose to have children. This is where it gets to the point where something needs to change. Which is why I am here.

We are all subject to these ancestral patterns and cycles to varying degrees and levels. Because we are all born of humans, who have also been exposed to this experience. What if I told you that you can consciously create the life *you* want rather than unconsciously pursuing a life you had no choice in choosing?

Now, please do not get me wrong, this is not an attack on those before us. This is about understanding how the human mind works and society is evolving. This is about understanding and appreciating our past so that we can understand our present moment. By understanding our past and present moment, we are given a very special gift that not enough people have... the freedom to consciously create our best life, the way *we* want to.

I truly believe it is no coincidence that we are only now coming into a new age of people consciously creating their best life. In the last thirty years, science has made some extreme revelations on how the world and humans work.

In the last ten year's there has been a huge uprising of people who are being awakened from their people pleasing patterning following slumber and experiencing extraordinary life transformations.

Words like energy, manifesting, consciousness and healing have become part of the normal vocabulary so many of us now frequently access. These words, that thirty years ago were shunned and thought of as malevolent, now come out of the proverbial closet as truth, possibilities and scientific proof.

You see, thirty years ago we were not equipped to do what so many of us are attempting to do today. Thirty years ago, we didn't have the knowledge and information that we possess today.

So, when people question me with why now? I reply, "*because we are undeniably ready and here's proof!*"

Which is precisely what I want to share with you. I want to share with you the proof that we now have the tools, skills and abilities to consciously create our best life. We now have access to infinite possibilities including health, wealth, success, freedom, love, connection, unity, peace, healing and so much more.

We now have choices to make and they can, for the first time ever, be choices we make solely for the purpose of making ourselves happy, joyful, and full of bliss. Because this new age of consciousness is not about pleasing others foremost anymore, and in turn depleting ourselves of precious energy and resources.

This new age of consciousness is all about empowering and

supporting the masses to utilise a power we were all born with through *The Conscious You*. A power that can transform any situation, any circumstance and any current reality that no longer suits our desires or serves a purpose in our life.

I can guarantee you that there is a power living stagnant inside you that is calling out to be activated and charged. A power that wants nothing but to obey your every wish and work with you to consciously create your best life.

You too can have everything you ever wanted! The experiences, materialistic things, emotional things and even the spiritual things. Whatever you want to achieve, or experience is yours to achieve and experience... all you need to know is what that power is, how to activate it, and how to use it to consciously create your most extraordinary life!

Before I share with you this power, I want to take a few quick minutes to remind you of what Alison shared earlier about what consciousness is, and now I'm going to go a little deeper.

Because without knowledge, we have no understanding. And without understanding, we have no power to create change in our life.

Now this is not to say that your life is horrible, and you are desperately seeking ways to change it. For some, this may be the case. For others, life may be good overall, and they just might be seeking that next level of success and happiness in their life.

Whatever you are seeking, please know that this power is available to everyone, no matter who you are or what you seek.

Well, I want to start by giving you facts. Scientifically proven facts about our subconscious and conscious mind.

Why is it so important that these facts be scientifically proven? Because science gives us recorded information that cannot be persuaded by the person conducting the experiment. Science is based on results that occur naturally and without human interruption.

Science is proof based information that is recorded while in its natural state and flow. That's not to say that everyone can have their own interpretation of this recorded information after the fact, but the recorded information itself must be untampered in order to be considered scientifically proven.

Which is why so many scientific experiments are conducted repeatedly and recorded thoroughly. Because science is not about interpretation, it's about facts, truths and realities at a point in time.

So then, let's look at some scientifically proven facts about consciousness.

Here we go... it has been proven that the human brain operates roughly 95% of the time on autopilot and only 5% on active thinking. Our conscious mind is the 5%. It's the active mind that is very aware and present in the moment. The subconscious mind is the 95% that runs on autopilot.

Science has shown that the conscious mind, at 5% operation, is the creative mind, the mind that has creative ideas, hopes and wishes. It's the imagination, the problem solver and the learner.

The subconscious mind is the mind that does most of our daily heavy lifting though. The subconscious mind is where all our beliefs, habits and behaviours are stored. For instance, how we brush our teeth, shower, put on our shoes and tie our shoelaces. It's also for things like do we chew our nails, smoke cigarettes, have a short fuse, or use sarcasm to mask our pain. The subconscious mind is where we store our beliefs such as religion, why we feel shame and guilt around particular things as well as political preferences etc.

As Alison shared earlier the subconscious mind is like a powerful hard drive that has had all these thoughts, beliefs, habits and behaviours downloaded into the memory of the computer, the same as if we would download different programs onto our computers at home.

The problem with the subconscious mind is, these programs continue to run in the background regardless of whether we want them too or not.

The way we eat is a perfect example of how dangerous the subconscious mind can be. So many of us struggle with emotional eating and overeating as a coping mechanism. And for the most part, we barely even notice we are doing it, until after the fact.

So, what happens is when we have a very difficult day, or a very emotional or traumatic experience, without even thinking about it, we find ourselves sitting in front of the television with food ready to numb our pain. It's not until the junk food is gone and the program you are watching finishes that we have a moment of clarity in which we feel guilty and shameful of our '*unhealthy*' coping mechanism.

Which then leads us into another downward spiral of autopilot beliefs around shame and guilt. Some of us feel the need to punish ourselves by starving our bodies or over exercising. Others of us feel the need to eat even more unhealthy food to numb the new pain we are feeling. Whatever it is we choose to do, it is all part of our autopilot programs at work. It happened subconsciously.

The bigger observation here is that in those brief moments of clarity, or in other words, moments of consciousness, we realise that what we are doing is '*wrong*' and '*unhealthy*', because we have no tools or knowledge of how to change said autopilot thoughts, beliefs, habits and behaviours, we automatically allow our subconscious programming to take control when we are not actively conscious.

We do this, not because we are weak, stupid, or scared but because we have no programming in our subconscious mind that supports a new way of doing things. We have no thoughts, beliefs, habits and behaviours that support a new way of dealing with pain when it comes up. We revert to old programming that is running on autopilot in our subconscious mind.

We have downloaded this programming from years of watching our elders as a child. Years of being conditioned to think, feel and act a certain way by our parents, schooling systems and the media to '*fit in*'.

Science says that from the time we are in our third trimester until the time we are roughly seven years old that we do not possess a conscious mind. We are unable to think consciously for ourselves. For those first seven and a bit years we are living and responding from our subconscious mind 100% of the time!

It is in our subconscious mind that we develop all our beliefs, thoughts, feelings, habits and behaviours. Because our subconscious mind is like a computer, it takes everything it learns, sees and hears and downloads this information as our basic programming. The more we learn, see and hear the same thing repeatedly, the more it becomes a fully functional and verified program in our subconscious mind.

That is why when we become adults ourselves, we find that we have so many similarities to those who raised us. Because up until the age of seven, in our imprint stage according to Morris Massey[1], we were a permanent sponge absorbing all the behaviours, habits and actions of those around us, informing us how we are to be in the world.

Imagine absorbing everything from those around us, what they would say, do, how they would behave and act. Our subconscious mind enables us to become miniature versions of the people we were surrounded by the most, and there was nothing we could have done about it.

This right here is your exception.

Now you know more. Now you know you have the knowledge and even perhaps the opportunity, to greatly impact and positively influence our next generation from the time they are in their third trimester.

What about those of us who have become fully grown adults? How can we reset, update or upgrade our subconscious programming? How can we take more of an active role in consciously creating our best life? And how can we tune into that 5% of our conscious programming more frequently?

So many great questions! And the best part is, I have found a way and I will share with you the solution, an incredibly powerful way to consciously create your best life. Before we discuss the nature of this solution it's important that you understand one thing.

The reason behind why the conscious mind is only able to operate 5% of the time is because the world is a busy place. Our world is noisy internally and externally. We think thousands of thoughts per second. We see and take in thousands of visions and images per second. Our conscious mind takes in so much information at once that it cannot possibly operate for longer than 5% of the time or our brains would overload, much like that of a computer, which can only store so much information.

That is why the subconscious mind, even though it can hold a lot of unhelpful or outdated thoughts, beliefs, habits and behaviours, is extremely powerful. It allows us to store relevant information and programming in our mind so that we can happen on autopilot, without having to think about every minute detail.

The human body is not yet evolved to function in this way,

where the conscious mind can be functioning for more time. Is there a possibility that this will change in the future? I believe so, anything is possible. And once you know the solution and have the tools to consciously create your best life, you will begin to experience a little more of this too.

Humans have a beautiful way of adapting and evolving. If you look at how science and medicine has evolved you will see how much of that is due to the human mind evolving, exploring and expanding. If science and medicine can make such profound and extraordinary progress, then so can you.

So, do you want to know what this powerful tool and solution is? Are you ready to embrace the science of it and apply it to your life? Are you ready to consciously create your best life as *The Conscious You*?

By all that is good and wonderful I hope you are screaming '*Yes*' in your head!

'*Yes*', because you have been wanting a better life for years. '*Yes*', because you have been feeling lost and confused and now want direction and purpose. '*Yes*', because you have felt out of alignment with yourself and are ready to live your life on purpose. '*Yes*', because you are tired of guessing and then second guessing every choice you make. '*Yes*', because you know there is more out there, you see so many other people experience more, and now you want more of what is out there too. '*Yes*', because you are tired of feeling shame, guilt, fear and confusion. '*Yes*', because you no longer want to live a stress-filled life, but one filled with joy, happiness and bliss.

I could go on and on and discuss all the amazing benefits to knowing how to consciously create your best life, but the truth is, only you could ever know what your heart desires. Only you can know what your soul craves. Only you could know what possibilities you want to experience. Only you can know what this next level version of yourself could be.

So why not take a moment to really feel into some of the possibilities you have only ever dreamed of. Take a moment to think about how they always seemed like distant dreams. And now, I want you to take a deep breath and consciously acknowledge that today could very well be the day that you finally get access to the powerful tool and solution to consciously create your best life. And that means every one of your possibilities has the potential to become your reality. Every single one of them!

You are about to learn what has changed my life in the most extraordinary of ways. You, are about to get access to information that is still so underground that most of the human civilisation has yet to hear about it.

Are you ready?

Let me begin by sharing some of my own journey and story so far. Why? Because some of you will relate to my journey and some of you will gain a deeper understanding of how powerful this tool and solution is when you realise what it has done for me.

So, let me start by saying this tool, this solution, has given me freedom.

Without going into all the ugly details of trauma, I want to share with you some of the emotional and mental turmoil I could heal, through learning this tool and solution. Because while our traumas may not be the same, often, the emotional and mental turmoil is similar.

Growing up, I experienced issues of abandonment, neglect, abuse, invisibility, loneliness, isolation and pain. Outside of these traumas there has always been issues with poverty, never feeling good enough or deserving enough, and always feeling guilt or shame around all the good things in my life.

Being human means, we are always striving for growth, happiness and ease. We want to experience more of what makes us feel good and less of what makes us feel bad. But we are having to deal with all these issues.

For me it meant that while growing up I attracted a lot of toxic and negative people into my life. Not all. No, not all. There are still some friends and some family who have stuck by me through the worst and the best of times. For the most part, there were a lot of people who came into my life that were there purely to serve a purpose, to teach me something. Not that I knew that at the time. At the time I was feeling frustration, anger, stress and helpless.

It's funny how everything seems so much clearer in retrospect.

I went through years of not knowing who I was and what my purpose was. My reality reflected my internal struggle as I spent years in toxic and unfulfilling jobs. I spent years dating toxic and damaged men who also had no idea of where they were going in life.

I also had moments of clarity. Clarity around my need to be independent. Clarity around my need to be and do more than I was doing. Clarity around my need to heal, let go of and transcend all past trauma so that I could live my life to its fullest potential.

More than ten years ago I started to embark on a journey of self-discovery that would lead me to the revelations that I am now about to share with you.

It was not a short journey and it sure is not a journey that is going to end anytime soon. In fact, I have come to realise that this journey of self-discovery and growth is one that will last my entire lifetime.

My journey started with the release of '*The Secret*' by Rhonda Byrne[2]. Within this book was this magical new way of thinking and manifesting my desires. I felt like I had finally found the missing key to my existence!

Of course! I can manifest everything my heart desires and create the life I truly want.

Ha! If only it were so easy, said in retrospect.

Over these ten years there was a massive increase in the amount of people and online coaches who claimed they could teach their craft of manifesting successfully. Everywhere you looked people were selling the dream!

The dream of consciously creating your best life through the art of manifestation. And for some, buying into these programs seemed to work. For me, not so much.

While I understood the concept and theory behind manifesting and consciously creating my best life, I continued to live in a constant state of traumatic pain, feelings of not being enough and old programming that kept me small and feeling damaged.

Have you ever felt like this? Like you know exactly what to do but no matter how hard you try to do exactly what you know to do, the past just keeps swinging around and slapping you in the face?

You promise yourself that you are going to dedicate yourself to eating better, exercising, being positive, not complaining, putting the laundry away as soon as it's dry, making the bed every morning and committing to your gratitude journal every day, but for some reason life always gets in the way.

Memories of not being good enough, smart enough, dedicated enough creep up and remind you that there's no point in making these commitments because it's only a matter of time before you realise, they will never work for you? This is what it was like for me.

Our subconscious mind, our human computer, never forgets a memory. Memories are part of forming our programming. If, for example, every time we ate ice cream our body released happy feelings, our subconscious mind would register this memory. Overtime our subconscious mind, through repetition of eating ice cream regularly, has a program now that tells us that we like to eat ice cream. Eating ice cream makes us happy.

When we are in a good mood or we need a pick me up, our

subconscious mind searches all our programs to find one that will allow us to continue feeling good or give us a boost. It often lands on, as per the example above, eating ice cream because we have all these memories of how eating ice cream has made us feel good.

Without even thinking, because our subconscious mind is on autopilot, we eat ice cream when we feel good and we eat ice cream when we feel bad in the hopes it will help us to feel good again. And I can tell you that I too have eaten a lot of '*ice cream*', while learning to figure this stuff out!

The same thing happens with our fear of failure. As children, we are taught that doing the right thing will land us applause and rewards while doing the wrong thing will lead to disappointment and punishment.

When we go to school we are graded by our academic performance and when we get good marks we are praised and rewarded while when we get bad marks we feel like a failure and feel disappointment.

All these instances are creating memories that then turn into our subconscious programming that runs on autopilot.

Now, when people, including me, talk about how they don't know why they are so fearful of failing, I light up and get excited because I know why!

Our programming has taught us to be so afraid of failing and doing the wrong thing that, when we become adults, we slowly stop taking risks. We slowly stop speaking our truth. We slowly start getting comfortable in doing what we are good at even if we hate it because there is no chance of failure. And failure means disappointment.

For me, learning this for the first time was like lifting the weight of the world off my shoulders. Understanding how the subconscious mind works literally was the start of a new beginning, a new consciously created life!

I began to recognise the patterns and programming that were a part of me. This awakening led to a new-found awareness and I started to notice when I reverted to my programming.

However, this alone didn't help me to change anything. This didn't lead me to freedom. Knowing and being aware is only the first step, not the last.

For years I thought I had found the key to being able to change my reality and consciously create my best life, yet nothing in my life had changed.

With this knowledge, all that was different was that now, more than ever, I was painfully aware of what I needed to change but had no idea of how to do it. To me, it was almost more painful than the actual issues I was dealing with. Knowing what the problem was, but not knowing the next step.

Have you ever felt that? Like the solution is just in the realms of your next step, but you don't know what that is?

Let's fast forward to 2019. This was meant to be my year of self-love. This was going to be the year that healed all my past traumas and healed all my issues. This was going to be the year that I learnt to love myself for who I am and then create a beautiful future of success, love and adventure!!

The year started out as a flop. I had good intentions but how the hell was I supposed to love myself exactly? I carried so much pain in my programming, it was with me everywhere I went. I carried so many issues that were part of my subconscious programming that it was so hard to love myself.

When I looked in the mirror, I saw a damaged woman. A woman who ate to numb her pain. A woman who was carrying way too much weight and misery in her face to be loved. And I repeatedly did the worst thing anyone could ever do on their journey of healing and self-love, I compared myself to everyone else.

Now I know that you've compared yourself to others, we have all done it at one time or other, it's something I know we can all relate to. The media, social media, schooling systems and government practices guarantees that you have compared yourself to someone else at least once in your lifetime!

This is so damaging and can completely undo any progress we make. And for me, it completely unravelled all the progress I had made over the last ten years.

I was left an empty shell of who I was. Not that it mattered because I didn't really know who I was anyway. I was merely a collection of memories and programs that told me I wasn't good enough and I'll never be worthy of what my heart desires. You could say I hit a very dark low. I felt very alone, even with the world's most supportive and loving fiancé a girl could ask for.

I felt lost, confused and hopeless. I had many long days and nights of sitting in front of the television, eating crappy food, trying to numb my pain. I didn't want to think about it because I knew I didn't have a next step, a solution. So, I avoided my pain all together.

After a few days of being completely numb, I took some time to reconnect with my spirituality for a few moments. I always believe the universe has my back but sometimes I need to step away from the universe and wallow for a bit. Which is what I did. I wallowed.

I don't know about you, but those people who never address the difficult emotions and just tell me to be positive and that there are other people in the world who have it worse than me can kiss my butt! For real.

It's not about feeling sorry for myself, it's about allowing myself to feel the realness of what I'm going through. And what I was going through was difficult! So, I wallowed dammit and did not feel a drop of shame or guilt. Once I felt like I could come up for some air, I had a short conversation with the Universe and my guardian angel, my father, that has changed my life forever!

I asked the Universe and my guardian angel to take over. I explained that I really had no idea how to heal and move forward from this place but what I knew was that I was tired of feeling like this. I was tired of having the same emotions, memories and issues come up repeatedly. I was tired of being this version of myself.

And for the first time in my life, I let go of control and expectations.

I didn't then start looking for signs from the universe, I just kept wallowing. I didn't then start checking the time and asking why it wasn't happening, I just kept wallowing.

And it wasn't until a few days later that I got the first nudge from the Universe.

I was wallowing on the couch when I randomly remembered that I had a subscription to what they call the spiritual version of Netflix; Gaia[3]. I had bought the Gaia subscription well over a year ago but had hardly spent any time on there. I went to my laptop and logged into Gaia not knowing exactly what I was looking for. Again, I released the control and expectations and just scrolled the recommended section until something sparked my interest. And sparked my interest did it ever.

I hereby proclaim my undying gratitude to Gregg Braden of '*Missing Links*'[4] for forever changing my life!

What started out as mild curiosity turned into learning the tool and solution to heal old programming and issues as well as consciously creating my best life.

What I'm about to share with you next is not my discovery. It is a collection of information, knowledge and research I have collated and put into use, which has changed my life.

What I am about to share with you is researched and proven science. And how I am about to explain it and share it with you is my interpretation. It is how I understand the years of

Quantum Physics and human biology research and case studies that have been performed by others. It's based on my own experience with the information and knowledge I have come into contact with.

You can take my interpretation of this tool and solution and apply it to your life, or you can embark on your own journey of Quantum Physics and human biology and come up with your own interpretation.

Let me introduce you to what I call Energetic Communications.

Energetic Communications is the tool and the solution that has allowed me to become this new, and incredible version of myself that I am so damn in love with! Energetic Communications is allowing me to actively heal all old and outdated programming that no longer serves a purpose. Energetic Communications literally saved my life and I am sharing it all here in the hopes that it can change and save your life too.

Here is what I have come to know when it comes to consciously creating your best life.

Everything is energy, absolutely *everything*. When you zoom in on anything you will always find that the smallest particle is always a photon, which is energy. Energy that is measured by the light it carries or the electromagnetic energy it emits. It is not a solid particle but an energetic one. And all things, including humans, when zoomed in on, are made of photons, energy.

It has been proven that even the empty space around us and around buildings and nature is also made up of energy. If I were to stand a metre away from a tree and there was nothing solid between us, like a large rock or flowers etc., some would say that there is an empty space between me and the tree. That is not true. Science and quantum physics have proven that there is an invisible force field of energy that exists everywhere. We are part of that force field, there is no empty space in our world or universe that is not part of this force field.

Everything and everyone are connected through this energetic force field. And this energetic force field is constantly accepting and delivering information and data that is constantly being emitted, by *everything*.

Here is the other thing that I know to be true, everything is communicating with everything all the time.

Think about this for a second. If everything is energy and energy is always moving and sending information and data, it means that we are in a constant state of communication. We are constantly communicating through the energetic force field that we are a part of, whether we know it or not.

Which means, when you look around at your current reality and you feel unhappy or unsatisfied or even say things like, "*I didn't ask for this*!" Science and Quantum Physics tells us that actually, you did.

I'm not saying that you *intentionally* wanted to create whatever in your life you might be unsatisfied with such as poverty, illness or toxic relationships etc. I know you would never intentionally do this! I never intentionally asked for the past traumas of my life or the issues I dealt with to be a part of my reality either. But they were.

The hardest thing to realise is that everything we do, think, feel, believe, is constantly reflecting to us through our current reality. Because most of what we do, think, feel, and believe is done automatically through our subconscious mind. It is a part of our automatic subconscious programming, which means it is running in the background and we are unaware of it. And while these programs are running in the background, they are communicating information and data into the energetic force field.

When we are communicating with the energetic force field (which is all the time) the force field automatically starts sending out signals into the field to try and find what it is you are communicating.

When you repeatedly say, "*I don't want to be in debt anymore*", the first thing that happens is your programming finds the memories of every time you were in debt. *Then*, the force field sends out signals to try and find you opportunities to continue to be in debt. Because it reads your communication as you wanting to continue to *feel* like you don't want to be in debt anymore. So, let's give you circumstances and situations where you can continue to feel like you don't want to be in debt anymore.

Suddenly, you get a massive electricity bill, or you get into a car accident, or you get sick and need to stay in hospital for a week, or your kid gets sick and you have to take a week of unpaid work leave. BOOM! You have just experienced Energetic Communication at its worst.

For me, I was always repeating that I needed to lose weight, I needed to make more money, I needed to heal my trauma, I needed more friends over and over again. And without even realising it I was always finding myself putting on more weight, so I continuously felt like I needed to lose weight. I found myself always being short of enough money, so I was always in a position where I felt like I needed more money. I was constantly having traumatic flashbacks so that I could feel like I needed to heal. And I was always struggling to make new friends so that I could feel like I needed to have more friends.

This is what makes Energetic Communication so powerful. It obeys your every distinct communication whether you want it to or not.

So, how can we upgrade our current level of Energetic Communication so that we can be honest to goodness, consciously creating our best life?

Simply put, we start by valuing, respecting and honouring our 5% of consciousness and active and present thinking, and experiencing what we currently have.

If we are to consciously create our best life, then we *need* to really appreciate and utilise the 5% of conscious living that we do get. Because if we can master the art of *Conscious* Energetic Communication we can heal and/or delete old subconscious programming that no longer serves us and create new subconscious programming that does serve us, and actively and consciously create our best life.

The solution here is Energetic Communication.

Before I share the process and practice I use, and have used to consciously create my best life, I want to give you true transparency. This is not a one-time deal; this is not an instant cure with lifetime benefits. This is a process and a practice that only gets better, faster and stronger with continued and consistent use!

In other words, embrace this tool and include it in your daily practices. And the more frequently you embrace this tool, the quicker your reprogramming occurs and the quicker you can consciously create your best life. And here is the added bonus, our ability to master the art of Energetic Communication means we can constantly level up our best life. We can live in a constant state of evolution, growth, prosperity, health, adventure and more. It doesn't have to stop once we reach a certain point, unless we want it to. This tool can be used every day for the rest of your life and will only get easier and faster to use.

Just think about a time when you had to learn something new, like how to ride a bike or drive a car. At first, it was rigid and mechanical, and you really had to concentrate. Then the more you practiced, the easier it got. And soon, it became part of your automatic subconscious programming and now you never have to think about it, you just do it.

The same applies for Energetic Communication. So, here are

the stages of appreciating and actively practising Energetic Communication as *The Conscious You.*

Awareness

Now you know that everything is energy and we are communicating all the time. You also know that our subconscious mind is automatically running all our programs in the background. Regardless of whether the program is good, bad or detrimental, it's running.

Understanding

Now you understand that your subconscious mind is creating most of your current reality, roughly 95% of it actually. Your subconscious programs are constantly energetically communicating with your energetic force field, and the energetic force field is constantly looking for situations and circumstances to deliver on what you are communicating.

Commitment

This is the commitment to taking daily conscious action to fine tune *your* Energetic Communications and the reprogramming of your subconscious mind.

Deletion

This is the stage where we actively participate in changing our communication, energetically consciously so that our subconscious can start to download updated programs, intentional programs that work for us!

Firstly, get into a state of consciousness and become present.

No distractions, no thinking about what to make for dinner or the list of 'to-dos' you need to get through.

Next, you need to acknowledge and recognise one program or 'issue' that you want to delete from your subconscious mind without judgement. What does that mean? It means that we select a program or issue we want to delete without malice, without thinking about how it has affected us up until this point, detached from the triggers and emotions that we are currently predisposed to subconsciously. We simply need to acknowledge that there is a program or issue that we are consciously choosing to delete. It doesn't matter if it's good, bad, right or wrong. It doesn't matter what memories it has created for us. There must be no judgement or labelling of this program or issue, simply acknowledge it exists and then acknowledge that you are about to consciously delete it from your subconscious mind.

To delete old programs or issues that no longer serve us we must not have any emotional attachment. We must not have any attachment at all. Remember, we are always communicating into the energetic force field and we want our communication about this program or issue to be one of detachment. One of no memories. One of no emotions. That way the data and information that we communicate into the energetic force field will be neutral and not cause a ripple effect of unwanted circumstances and situations.

Once you have the program or issue you are going to delete selected, you are going to complete a visualisation I developed with the help of the Universe and my guides.

- When you are ready you will close your eyes, put your hand on your heart and breathe deeply. In through your nose for five seconds and out through your mouth for five seconds.
- Repeat this until your mind and body become calm. When we close our eyes and complete deep and extended breathing - we tell our mind and body that we feel safe in this moment and our fight or flight hormones relax and we feel calm.
- If you ever feel distracted or anxious while doing the breathing, focus on the hand over your heart. Focus on your hand going up and down with your breathing. Once you are feeling relaxed you will find you automatically return to breathing in and out of your nose slowly.
- Now, with your eyes still closed, this is where I want you to visualise that your mind is a computer. I want you to imagine a computer screen where your brain is.
- On that computer screen is your current desktop, image one folder.
- Under the one folder is written in capital letters; PROGRAMS
- I want you to imagine moving the mouse under your hand so that the cursor on the screen hovers over the folder.
- Double click the folder using the left button of your mouse.
- Inside the PROGRAMS folder are three more folders. Under the first folder it says ACTIVE. Under

the second folder it says INACTIVE. Under the third folder it says OUTDATED.

- I want you to click on the OUTDATED folder and open it.
- When the OUTDATED folder opens what you find is a list of outdated programs that are still running subconsciously. Outdated because they are harmful, hurtful or have stopped serving a purpose.
- I want you to scroll the list until you find the outdated item that matches the program you selected at the beginning of this process.
- Once you find the outdated item, I want you to look across the screen to the right, at the end of the outdated item is a red button that reads DELETE PROGRAM.
- I want you to press that red button.
- Once you've pressed the red button a small screen pops up that asks you; Are you sure you want to DELETE this program?
- Underneath this question are two buttons. One button reads; NO, I'M NOT READY. The other button reads; HELL YES - DELETE THIS PROGRAM NOW!
- I want you to click on the button that reads; HELL YES - DELETE THIS PROGRAM NOW!
- A new screen pops up that reads; Confirmed - program deleted.
- Congratulations, you have just deleted an old subconscious program that was taking up space.
- Smile, take a deep breath and open your eyes.

Here is what I believe to be the good news, you only ever need to delete a program once. If you continue to delete the same program over and over, you are once again sending out very clear Energetic Communication. And that Energetic Communication is that this is a program that needs to continue existing so that you can continue to delete it. Which means the energy force field will keep finding you situations, circumstances or memories to reinforce that you *do* need to delete this program, over and over again.

Let's *not* go through that loophole experience.

So, how can we create a new and improved program to replace the old one that we just deleted?

New Programs

This is the most powerful way you can now consciously create your best life as *The Conscious You*. This is where you create a possibility of what your new programming could be. Let me share one of my experiences to help explain what I mean.

An old program that I deleted was that I was a victim. A victim of past traumatic experiences. Once I had deleted this program, I then went about creating a list of possibilities for what my life could look and feel like now that I was no longer a victim.

Some of the possibilities included letting go of all resentment, anger and frustration towards the people who played a part in my traumatic past. Another possibility was feeling complete freedom in the choices I make. Feeling calm and collected. Feeling joy and happiness.

What I did next has been the most beautiful experience of consciously creating my best life. I took my list of possibilities and got into a conscious state. And I gave thanks and expressed gratitude for already experiencing these possibilities as actual realities in my current life.

For example; *"Thank you Universe for this freedom I feel every day"*. *"I am so grateful to be healed"*. *"I am so grateful that I feel calm, happy and joyful every single day"*. *"I truly am blessed"*.

My Energetic Communication started sending out data and information into the energetic force field to start collecting or creating situations or circumstances where I can continue to feel this new way of feeling.

Within moments of completing my Conscious Appreciation for what is already happening in my life, I felt joy and calmness like I'd never felt before. I felt free of all the resentment, anger and frustration. I felt like I could breathe, like I had the freedom to *be me*!

The process doesn't stop there. This is where practice begins. Every day, and as many times a day as I can, I get into a state of conscious appreciation for what is already happening in my life (the possibilities).

Every day my Energetic Communication is sending out information and data into the energetic force field that is then collecting and creating situations and circumstances to affirm that what I am consciously appreciating is indeed true.

When this becomes a repetitive practice, soon, just like learning to ride a bike or drive a car, it becomes a subconscious program. The subconscious mind develops programs through repetitiveness and habits. While the conscious mind can learn and create in the moment, what we learn and create cannot automatically become fully integrated into our subconscious mind. First, we need to experience repeated circumstances and situations where we can use our new creation or learned information to prove to our subconscious mind that indeed, this *is* a new program we need to upload.

Which is why knowing the power of Energetic Communication allows you to now consciously create circumstances and situations you want to experience.

With repetitive practice of conscious appreciation, over a period of time (for some this is days, others it's months, it depends on your level of commitment), you are no longer giving thanks for possibilities but experiencing these very possibilities as your reality. You have consciously created your best life all while healing your pains, deleting old programs that no longer serve you and learning the art of Energetic Communication.

Once you've deleted one program and successfully uploaded a new and consciously created program, you will realise just how powerful this tool and solution is to create your most magical life ever.

Phew. I honestly didn't know how I was going to relay all this powerful and juicy information to you, but I deleted my procrastination programming and started giving conscious appreciation for a chapter that brings joy, hope and excitement to every person who reads it!

I have given thanks for the amazing results every reader has experienced because of this shared information and now look where we are... At the end of a powerful chapter I didn't originally know how to write.

I consciously created my best chapter ever and I truly desire that it gives you a powerful and useful tool to consciously create your best life!

ABOUT SAMANTHA HADDAD

Samantha Haddad is a passionate and heart-centred entrepreneur, writer and soulful communications expert. She truly believes that life's most important skill is our ability to communicate effectively, soulfully, and from a place of love.

With a background in sales, management and leadership, Samantha has been studying human psychology, human emotion and human connection for over 15 years. Her vast experience as an observer, researcher and communicator has allowed her to build an incredible online audience where she shares her life's work.

As an entrepreneur, she has spent years supporting thousands of other entrepreneurs through her abilities as a conscious copywriter, content creator and communications coach.

She has empowered women all over the world to share their story, build their business and work with their soul clients all through her teachings on energetic and conscious communication and copywriting.

As a writer, her life's work is very much about helping women to find their empowered voice through their written and spoken words – their soul language. She believes that when we are able to communicate our truths, desires and beliefs in a soulful way, we are able to create a ripple effect of love, connection, growth and healing for ourselves and beyond.

Samantha has spent the last three years developing her own concept of energetic communications and is determined to spread the word through her efforts as a conscious and soulful entrepreneur, writer and soulful communications expert.

She believes that women hold the key to changing the way the world functions and that when women realise the power of their empowered and soulful voices, they'll use them, and the world will listen. Her hope is that she can enlighten as many women as possible to communicate in this new way so that they may experience and live their own conscious truths, freedom of choice and bliss.

E: samanthahaddad84@gmail.com

 facebook.com/Soulful-Communications-100154424725072

CONSCIOUS CONNECTION IS A SACRED INVITATION TO SHARE OF YOURSELF FOR WHAT MIGHT BE THE BRIEFEST OF MOMENTS. SO, MAKE IT COUNT, MAKE IT MATTER AND ABOVE ALL MAKE IT YOUR BEST.

YOUR IMPACT AND INFLUENCE EXPAND BEYOND THIS ONE CONNECTION, BE MINDFUL OF THE ENERGY YOU BRING AND THE OUTCOME YOU ARE SHARING

CONSCIOUS CONNECTIONS

BY BECK THOMPSON

'Relationships are part of our life force; we need human connection to thrive.

So, choose your connections consciously'.

I want to get really clear from the outset. Relationships are a choice. There are no relationships in your life that are forced upon you that you need to keep. It might feel that way sometimes, but it is not the truth. No family, work, friends or partners are there forever, unless you choose it to be that way.

Let me tell you a story, a flashback to my life about five years ago. I had a myriad of different friendships and it is something that I wore as a badge of honour. I would be constantly catching up with people and to be honest I spread myself very thin. There were times when my husband used to say to me that I put everyone else before him and I shrugged it off like he didn't know what he was talking about. It wasn't till I witnessed a very good friend say no to catching up with me because she needed to spend time with her husband and kids that the penny dropped. But the penny didn't drop instantly. First, I was offended as I completely did not understand this point of view, it was foreign to me, after a bit of reflecting I got it. I was putting everyone else above the relationship with my husband and most of all I was putting everyone else above my relationship with myself. It was from there on in I changed the way I did relationships and chose to consciously create and maintain the relationships that I truly wanted in my life.

The relationship lessons that I experienced from that point forward have steered my life in a different direction, they have made my relationships more fulfilling and connected. Although at times the lessons have challenged me, they have led me to grow in ways I am so grateful for. This is why I wanted to share these lessons with you, because if you can take away one learning and apply it, I can guarantee that you will have closer connections. Not only with those around you but with yourself too.

Let's straighten something else up. Relationships are in all areas of your life and although you can choose the relationships you have, if you are not present and aware you will find yourself participating in transactional relationships that you think you didn't choose. Being in a relationship is not exclusive to husband and wife etc. Every interaction you have with another human being is a chance to enhance a relationship or have it go the other way. That is why this chapter is not about a particular set of relationships but rather how to consciously create the most amazing relationships in all areas of your life and experience them to their fullest. Because you cannot consciously create your best life without intentionally and actively connecting to and choosing your best relationships.

All relationships require the same set of skills believe it or not. What is different is how you use those skills and what skills you use.

What does differ in each distinct relationship is how different people impact each other. For example, there are people in my life who push my buttons, and they could say the same thing as someone else to me and I would instantly feel different depending on the person. I would call these people trigger points.

Trigger points are something that take you back to a memory or a time in your life when someone/something had an impact on you. Trigger points are enacted by one of your five senses, so in terms of relationships it could be the way someone talks, could be the tone they use, the words they say, a certain smell or how someone looks. Often when someone triggers us, we are unaware of why, or even that they have triggered us, it is just that we feel a friction or frustration arise within us. The insights at the end of the chapter will help you get to understand yourself better, which will in turn help you to understand why certain people will likely trigger you and how you can stop that trigger from affecting you.

So, before we get into the steps to help you consciously create your ideal relationships, let me tell you a little bit about my story and why I love relationships so much. And why I want to teach the world how to have the best relationships across all areas of their life.

Let me give you an insight into what changed when I switched the way I viewed relationships.

I had noticed that after interactions with people I was either left feeling drained, feeling energised or feeling a bit 'meh'. If I felt drained or 'meh' it was a clear signal to me that I needed to cut down or stop the amount of time I spent with that person or be selective about when I did see them. For the interactions where I felt energised, I wanted to increase those. Now, this had absolutely nothing to do with if the person was feeling sad or happy on an occasion, it was more than that, it was how I felt energetically after an interaction with them. I actively now use this, my energetic compass, as my rule of thumb for who I hang out with and how often, so that I control with intention my relationships and energetics.

Life for me from a young age had me convinced that I would never get married as marriages end in divorce (as those were the only examples I had witnessed), and this was my story. I was also so stuck on the story that I was the way I was and if people didn't like that then that was their bad luck because I wasn't changing. Until it didn't work anymore. You see those ways of thinking that we get ourselves stuck in are so rigid that they leave no room for growth. The one thing that I was, even more so than the above stories, was determined! Determined to always have a better life and better relationships and to constantly improve them. So, here began my journey of reevaluating how I showed up in the world.

The starting point for me was when I put one foot into the world of personal development - it was scary, confronting, challenging - but oh so rewarding. Which is exactly what a new relationship is! Personal development opened my world and my eyes up to a place I had never been before. It was a place where I knew that I could be a better me and the place that first introduced me to the world of coaching to which I instantly fell in love. It also changed the way I viewed relationships, and I grew to know that if I wanted the relationships to improve in my life whether they were friendships, work colleagues, family or intimate relationships then I had to look at the part I played in them and take full responsibility for that part. By full responsibility, I mean owning everything you bring or don't bring to a relationship.

Often we focus on the other person. It is so much easier to blame and complain about the other person than it is to look at our own behaviours and change those. The issue with this viewpoint is that if we are focused on the other person then we do not stand a chance at the relationship improving, and we end up going around in circles. Think about how draining a relationship is if you are constantly having to have the same fights, the same annoyances and it just never ends! I would rather stab myself in the eye with a fork. It is easier to think... *"What could I change about me in this scenario to get the best out of the other person and enhance both of our lives?"*

However, it is fair to say that this is not an easy or consistent approach, well certainly not for me. There are times when I am not present, or I am tired and cranky. These times mean that I get more easily frustrated by others. So, as we go through how you can consciously create your best relationships remember that you are human and therefore you will not always get it 'right' and that is perfectly normal. If I have learnt one thing from the world of personal development it would be that when you get it 'wrong' (which is not a word I believe in, let's just use it in this context), the worst thing you can do is fall into guilt and shame. The reason nothing is ever 'right' or 'wrong' is that every situation brings a different outcome and each one was meant to be. So instead of falling into the guilt and shame of a decision, look at it as a learning opportunity, take it as a chance for growth. If you do this I promise you will find things shifting. Also remember, and this is an absolute belief of mine, that everyone including you is doing the best they can at any given moment. That best might look different day to day, even minute to minute, but it is absolutely your best, so give yourself a break.

I am now going to walk you through a number of stages designed to bring your awareness to the seven aspects that impact and influence your relationships. My hope is that you consider them and begin to consciously create your best approach to relationships and your contribution to them. The areas that we will go through in more detail are Communication, Emotional Intelligence, Boundaries, It's Not About You, Masculine and Feminine, Respect and All Emotions are Valid.

So, let me break these areas of awareness down and tell you

about how they came to serve me in my life and how I learnt about them.

Communication

Anyone who knows me well, knows that I could talk under water. In fact, it has taken me a long time to learn that I don't need to say everything that pops into my head and the power is actually in listening first and speaking last. Communication is something that I have always been interested in. From a young age I was fascinated in the way that different people communicated with each other and the different outcomes this would lead to. When I started studying social work and got to the section in my degree on therapy, I realised that I was so thirsty for knowledge about how to improve my communication that the desire to teach these concepts was created. The people around me then became part of my experiment (shhh don't tell them).

I began to practice changing the way I communicated with different people and witnessed the different outcomes that were achieved. I narrowed this down to a set of guidelines that work for me, and yet I must reiterate we are human and therefore not infallible. Relationships, and working on relationships is lifelong work and some days you get it 'right' and other days you most certainly do not, the more you can take responsibility for when you don't get it 'right' the faster the learning will be.

Emotional intelligence

A new buzz word for sure and we have all been practicing different parts of it for years. As Alison has already shared aspects of the importance of Emotional Intelligence (EI), let me summarise by saying that it is essentially the capacity to be aware of, control, and express our emotions. Emotional Intelligence in relation to connections, allows us to handle interpersonal relationships judiciously and empathetically. Learning about and practicing emotional intelligence for me came about when I entered the incredible, steep learning curve of personal development. Becoming aware of myself, my triggers and my reactions to people, situations and places. My first experience of personal development was a weekend course on Personal Success. A course that opened my mind and challenged me to expand. Most of all I felt alive. I caught the feeling of growth and my mind expanding. This was the beginning of many courses for me and they became addictive. The high you are on when you leave these courses is like no other and as I began to do them with my husband I fell even more in love with them. The trick to that lasting feeling of expansion was to ensure I implemented my learnings when I wasn't in the course environment!

It certainly hasn't come naturally to me to be aware of my behaviours and patterns, nor have I been present enough all the time to practice these skills with sound judgement and sense. There are absolutely still times that people frustrate the shit out of me and let me tell you I am not the most patient person when it comes to some people, but it's a process of self-awareness and evolution and sometimes it is one step forward two steps back and that is ok, because even during reflection you are still going forward.

. . .

Boundaries

Boundaries are so interesting and something I have had to learn about later in life. We learn about boundaries from around the age of two to three and often rebel against them. Boundaries are what make us feel safe. An area I have focused on with my boundaries is my time. And by time, I mean the time that I give people and the time that I give myself. This lesson I learnt from my husband. The balance very much used to be that I would give people 95% of my time and allow myself 5% of my time (isn't it funny how those percentages land in the exact subconscious and conscious predispositions!). I always regarded it as a good thing and something to be proud of that I put my friendships first. As I have grown older that balance has shifted to dedicate more time to me and my closest relationships, but it wasn't easy. When my husband used to give me the feedback that I did too much for others I would get defensive and regard him as selfish as he wasn't doing what I regarded as the 'right thing'. There wasn't a precise trigger for this learning, and it was something I was quite stubborn in changing but over time my priorities changed. Like anything, there are times when I still fall back into this habit but now I know it is not sustainable and for me it actually leads to burnout which I do not tolerate. Sacrificing yourself for the good of others is not noble, it doesn't make you a saint or selfless it makes you non-existent and in the long run you will be no good for anyone, not even yourself.

It's not about you

This is not meant to be an insult but more of a reminder to not take things so personally. The learning for this came into my life the same way the learning for emotional intelligence did and it came with the learnings of personal development and working on and constantly improving myself. My lesson for this came one day when I heard someone saying, "*you don't have to say everything that is in your head*". It wasn't directed at me, I remember thinking, '*OMG I say everything that is in my head, often when it has no relevance*'. It was as though my self-worth was tied to me getting all my knowledge out in every interaction with people, I needed them to know how much I knew. What a revelation! From this point forward I remember thinking, '*you have two ears and one mouth for a reason, if you just stop talking you might be able to learn something from others*'. It was also following this journey of expansion that led me to learn not to take things personally and that the world didn't revolve around me. I learnt that everyone has their own stuff going on and their behaviour, words and actions is more a reflection of them than it is of me.

It is, however, still something I must constantly remind myself of whenever I get offended by, or upset at someone's actions, or words. Trust me once you realise that everyone is doing the best they can at any given moment, and this can vary from moment to moment, life becomes a hundred times easier and your stress level drops dramatically.

Masculine and Feminine energy

This is a very new learning for me but also one that I consider the most valuable of my life so far. For the majority of my life I have led and had relationships where I was coming from a masculine energy. My lessons from my journey of working in the relationships field is that it is very common for women to come from this masculine energetic space. For me it would be that I was and still am at times very assertive, controlling, confrontational etc. When I learned to lead from and be in my feminine energy I became more understanding, intuitive, and compassionate. I know when I am in my feminine energy as I am in complete flow. When I am trying to force an outcome or avoid a situation I am usually in my masculine state. I have found that life works best for me when I lead from my feminine energy. Does that mean that I am no longer assertive? Absolutely not. Through engaging The Conscious You, it is the way that I am assertive and the tone that I use that makes all the difference now.

Respect

Respect is something that was drilled into me from a young age and it is something that I have always done to people's faces but not always behind their back, which is not something I am proud of but something I continue to work on. My biggest learning in respect was when I started working in a youth centre, it was my first job in a social work field and I soon learnt that if I didn't give the kids the same respect I wanted from them then I wasn't going to be able to make any connection or impact. I had to start by being what I wanted in order to make a change and model respectful behaviours. I think we often get taught to respect our elders, but respect should be to and from everyone, not just those you deem in a hierarchy of position or age. It is fundamental in being with others.

. . .

All Emotions Are Valid

For so much of my life I was a rescuer, if I saw someone in pain or in what I deemed to be a negative emotion I would want to save them and get them out of it. Let me tell you something, this was all about me and how I felt about those emotions, not the other person. When you pull someone out of those necessary emotional states you don't allow them to have the full experience to grow, you stop them from coming full circle with the experience, it also sends a strong signal that not all emotions are ok. That is completely false, all emotions are valid and necessary. Because of this I sometimes struggle with calling them 'negative' and 'positive' emotions as it implies that one is bad, and one is good.

Sadness is just as important as happiness and you need to experience the rain to have the sunshine. It is all well and good for me to say this now, but sadness is an emotion that I have not always been comfortable with, in fact I would go as far to say that I avoided it every chance I got. I remember being upset at a school camp and a friend came up to me and said, "*why are you crying, you're not allowed to be sad, you are always the happy one*". Which confused me and made me angry, but it ultimately became part of my identity. The older I grew the more I avoided sadness and I took on this belief that because I had held it in for so long if I were ever to become sad I wouldn't know how to make it stop and I would be stuck in a sad place forever. The thought of that was unbearable.

Because I was so uncomfortable with sadness, and I had created this belief I would not allow anyone else around me to be sad, or angry or frustrated. This became my coping mechanism and methodology, avoidance and distraction. Eventually, on my personal development journey and through working with a therapist and a coach, I learnt to sit with my own emotions, the whole spectrum of them until I could understand and accept them all. Then eventually I sat with other people in their emotions and I allowed them to experience their emotions to the fullest and they didn't have any affect over me. I see all emotions as such a valuable part of life.

Now that you have brief insight into how I began to be impacted by my relationships and how I categorised these seven incredibly powerful aspects of relationship building and understanding. I want to give you the tools to put these aspects to work for you so that you can start to bring your awareness to *The Conscious You*, and you too can start creating your best relationships.

Communication

Communication is so much more than we think it to be, case in point Samantha's chapter on Energetic Communication, right? In fact, 70% of communication is nonverbal. So, when we are speaking to someone and thinking that our words are being misunderstood we forget to realise that it might be the way that we are saying it, it might be the time and place that we are saying it in, for example if I am to talk to my husband whilst he is watching TV, it frustrates him - one because he is trying to focus on one thing and I am then asking him to switch automatically to listen to me for something else and secondly this is his time to switch off. I therefore need to think about the time and place I discuss matters in. If it is urgent and I need to talk to him, I might say *"hey babe, I know you're in the middle of watching tv, there is something really important I'm wanting to talk to you about, would it be ok if you paused that for a minute?"*

Even though the verbal component only makes up 30%, those words we use are really important and often underestimated. Language is key.

So how can you improve your communication skills? Well besides the fact that a whole book could be written on this, I'll give you my top line skills;

- **Think before you speak** - Don't just blurt out whatever is on the top of your head without taking time to process what you are going to say and the impact this is going to have on the other person/people. This becomes more difficult the more heated a conversation can get, because as emotion rises, intelligence falls. So, it is a skill that needs to be practiced over and over again and perhaps during those heated times, it is actually a good time for you to walk away, have a breather, and then return to say what you need to say.
- **Not everything that is in your head needs to be said.** Trust me, it took a while for me to learn this skill, I used to think that everything I had to say was the most important thing in the world. Then I began to learn the complete opposite. The

moment I shut up and began to listen to other people, my world became so much richer, I learnt so much. Remember that we have two ears and one mouth for a reason.

- **Listen** - and I mean really listen. All the time in coaching I hear people say that they don't really feel heard by the other person. This comes down to many factors but one of them is that often people spend the time they are not speaking in the conversation, thinking about what they are going to say next. Now, I know we are clever creatures us human beings, but you really cannot hear what the other person is saying if you are having a whole conversation with yourself in your own head, can you?
- **Tone** - *"it is not what you said, it's how you said it"* - have you heard or said this before? That is because the way you say something is often more important that what is being said. Tone refers to the quality of the voice you use. If you are getting a negative response after you have spoken to people, then take a moment to reflect on what you said and how you said it and ask yourself, could either of these be changed?

Emotional Intelligence

The level of your emotional intelligence will directly correlate to the quality of your relationships. Emotional intelligence refers to the ability to identify, manage and express one's own emotions, as well as the ability to be able to understand, interpret and respond to the emotion of others. The reason this is so key is that often in relationships different people trigger us in different ways, when we get triggered we automatically respond in a certain way, until we learn to manage those triggers and the emotions that are formed from them. Having higher emotional intelligence gives you the ability to manage your relationships better and get the best from others and yourself even when you are faced with conflict.

In a day we can go through about sixty to seventy emotions, most of them you won't even register or fully experience and a lot of them, I can safely say are not the ideal ones to consciously create your best relationships. A lot of us believe that emotions control us, and we have no control over them and will often blame others for how we feel. I know I have said to people in the past "*stop it you're making me angry, sad, etc.*". When the truth is that no one can make us feel anything. Realising this can be the most freeing thing because it gives us the power to know that we are in charge of our emotions and we can choose the ones that we use.

As I guide you through some ways to build on your Emotional Intelligence in order to improve your internal and external connections, you will start to notice that there are patterns and habits that you fall into effortlessly and there are certain emotions that you use on a regular basis. The purpose of these strategies is for you to become more self-aware and conscious of how you are feeling in situations throughout your day, and around certain people so you can begin to strengthen your emotional intelligence muscle.

- **Journal** - Journaling enables you to get to know

yourself and your triggers. The more you get to know yourself and the emotional responses you have, the more you will be able to recognise and label your emotions. Journaling can be a great way to get to know yourself, simply start by putting pen to paper and write whatever comes up for you, it doesn't have to make any sense, and no one needs to read it. By putting your thoughts out there on paper you will begin to raise your awareness of the different emotional states you find yourself in.

- **Awareness** - Begin to become aware of your feelings and emotions as you go through the day. When you notice that you have become angry or sad or frustrated, stop and have a think about what was happening before, during and after that moment. At first you might not realise until the next day or a few hours after the event, then as you practice this skill you might notice just after the event, and soon enough you will be able to notice yourself in the middle of the emotional reaction and you might even be able to pause and question what is happening to enable you to change the direction the interaction is headed.
- **Remember to Breathe** - Just as you begin to become aware of emotions and feelings, work on consciously taking a breath before you respond as it will give you time to think and feel if it is the best response for the time. If you work on practicing more mindfulness in your life this will also help you to slow down and remind you to take that breath. You will

start to see how your body slips into that habit of quiet connection and contemplation of breath especially when processing certain triggers and emotions, and the benefit this strategy alone can have on you is profound.

- **Physical Reactions** - Become aware of your physiological reactions, for example what you feel in your physical body in regard to situations, people or places. When we can become aware of the symptoms that occur in our body, in alignment with our emotions, we can improve our self-awareness and better understand and manage our emotions. Just like becoming aware of your feelings and emotions this awareness might not happen straight away but with practice it will. What you are looking for are physiological responses such as a racing heart, sweaty palms, talking fast etc. Tuning into your subconscious and habitual responses and acknowledging them, will help pave the way for you to get into the emotional and physical state that will assist you in improving your response to your physical signals.
- **Reminder you are not your Emotions** – Key time to remember that as Alison said earlier, you are not your emotions, create this belief, align with it and know the power in the experience as emotions pass through *The Conscious You*.

Boundaries

Boundaries are so important in all relationships not just that of an intimate nature, particularly if you want healthy thriving relationships, and here's why.

Boundaries are your way of saying to someone this is where I begin and end. I am sure you have got on a plane and in the safety instructions they say put your own mask on before you help others. Setting clear and healthy boundaries helps you communicate more effectively what is important to you and acceptable for you, while making conflict less likely to occur when this information is known. Boundaries also support you to not burn out and therefore keep your relationships healthier for longer. Setting clear boundaries does not have to be difficult but it does require a level of self-respect and it is important to not only set the initial boundaries but to keep them. That doesn't mean that the goal posts can't change, but if you go from doing one thing to another to another and allowing different types of behaviours, it can become confusing for those around you and they will be unclear how to treat you, which means that your boundaries become blurred.

Starting to implement boundaries with existing relationships can often ruffle some feathers and create some conflict as your people are used to you acting in a certain way. The key here, is to be consistent with the boundary you want to create, while explaining the need you have for this to be your new normal, and why it is important to you, whilst acknowledging that the other person might want to have a better understanding.

This is how I choose to set clear boundaries with others, and highly recommend the process. As you will see, there is far more inner work than external work to be actioned initially. As with all communication, it starts with us, so;

- Get clear on what your needs are, and clearly communicate those needs with others. It is your responsibility to let others know what you need, not for them to guess what your needs are and how you like to be treated.
- Get to know yourself as a person. This is related to the emotional intelligence piece and once you get to know what you will and won't tolerate, it is about holding those boundaries firm and communicating them with others.
- Use '*I*' statements to communicate with others around how you are feeling. An example of an I statement would be: "*I would like it if you let me know that you are coming over so I have time to prepare*". The opposite of an I statement would be if you say, "*you make me feel*" or "*you need to do this*". '*I*' statements communicate that you are taking personal responsibility and ownership rather than blaming others.
- Be direct and clear with people. This combines points 1 and 3 above. An example of this might be, "*I want to hear your question, right now I am in the middle of something, if you come back in 10 minutes I can give you my full attention*"

The importance in all of this, is that the more you get to know yourself and the more you value your self-worth, the easier it will be to set boundaries with people. Trust me, people both respect and crave boundaries, particularly those that push them the most.

It's not About You

I know a few of you might be reading this and thinking what? It's not about me, everything is about me surely? We are taught that personal development is an inward journey, so why would this approach be included if we were sticking true to that. Well because we often forget that other people are human too, and what I mean by that is that everyone has a history and everyone has conditioning that has led them to be the person they are today, which might be a very different person than you. There are so many beautiful things about diversity and yet we often struggle with those that are most different to us. This isn't about taking onboard their differences or seeing them as more important, it is literally the action of awareness that the way other people are, is not always as a result of us. So, withdrawing the personal response mechanism makes way for curiosity of another, and what led them to this place, to this person, to this perception. The funny thing is the world would be so boring if everyone around you were the same, I know at times we think this would be the solution to so much but here are my thoughts.

Meeting new people, and people we consider different to us, have so much to teach us about how they see the world and the different views they have.

When someone unknowingly triggers you, it often leads to us

taking personal offence and it really is not about you. Try switching the lens which you see them through, from assumptions or judgement to curiosity and kindness, which is a mindful approach. Remember it's not about you, you do not have the power to make someone feel anything, so you are absolved of responsibility for another, and now can get back to the internal work and wonderment of another's journey.

I have listed some things for you to consider, to help expand your thinking on this.

- **Start with Compassion** - Have compassion for others, everyone has a whole life running behind the scenes which you won't always know about. Remember to be kind and curious, because generally when people hurt other people they are hurt and therefore need love not hurt in return.
- **Triggers** - Everyone triggers someone, there will always be someone (if not a few people) in life that trigger you and you trigger. This is because everyone has a history and different traumas that have happened to them over their lives. When you are triggered think about the strategies you have to acknowledge your emotions, and when you trigger someone else consciously practice dropping into empathy and compassion.
- **Empathy** - Practice having empathy for others. The way I like to describe empathy is to put yourself in the other person's shoes, walk a day in their life. This is very different to sympathy where you are feeling sorry

for someone. Instead of feeling sorry for them you think about their life and situation and imagine what it would be like, this will give you some insight into why they might be feeling the way they are feeling and why they are acting in a certain way, it will also allow compassion to come into play.

Masculine & Feminine approaches to Relationships

Right now, it feels to me as though the world is a little out of whack in relation to this energetic approach. We have women mainly leading from their masculine and men mainly being in their feminine and in my opinion, it just doesn't work as it is not naturally where we are designed to live from.

How this plays out in life is that you have women leading from their masculine and being in charge of everything from the finances, to the cleaning, to the parenting, this leaves little space for the man to be in their masculine and take charge. This way of being often frustrates women and they try and make the man change, what they don't realise is that if they are taking up all the space doing everything it leaves no room for him to step into the role they so desperately want. To do this, the space needs to be left and the feminine in her flow needs to step in, not giving direction or bossing the masculine around but allowing. This doesn't mean you should exclusively have feminine energy if you are a female and vice versa but I want you to experiment living with a balance of your feminine state being semi dominant and see if you notice a difference in your relationships. Here is how you can allow your feminine to start leading through *The Conscious You*;

- **Let it go** - When you feel yourself getting stuck or trying to force a situation, focus on letting go of the outcome. You have done all you can on your end to make it happen so now, it's up to forces larger than you to allow it to happen if it is meant to. Holding on too tightly will suffocate it, so let go and be in flow.
- **Use your intuition** - Women have such strong intuition and gut feelings about what the best path for them is. Do you ever recall that absolute knowing that something was about to happen, and then boom, it did? That tingle, that inner voice, that feeling of connection, however you experience it, that is your spark of intuition. Sometimes this comes into effect when women become mothers, sometimes before, sometimes after, however you start to feel connected with it, know it has in fact always been there, you might just need to notice and work with it more now. I invite you to work with this feeling, this spark, next time you are questioning what you should do, get still and quiet. You absolutely have the answer within, you don't need to search, research just listen to your intuition. Trust its tell; it is always right.
- **Slow down and practice being present** – This is when you can allow the feminine energy to step up. To be present start to focus on your five senses, they will automatically bring you in to the

moment. Stop and focus on what you can see, smell, hear, feel and taste. Another way to be in the moment is to focus on your breath. Practice breathing in for four counts, holding your breath for a moment and breathing out for four counts, in that moment all you can focus on is your breath and it will bring your heart rate right down. A slower heart rate is more synonymous with the free flow of the feminine energy, so you will start to feel that rise.

- **Get creative** - The feminine is all about creativity and play. Have a think back to when you were young, what did you enjoy doing? Painting, dancing, or singing? Bring back that creative side and watch the feminine flow come back into your life.

Respect

Respect means something different for everyone, and often it means different things in different relationships. I believe that respect in a healthy relationship means that both parties in the relationship are equal, sure the roles might be different such as in an employer boss situation but that does not mean that you are not equals and that the behaviors, manners, kindness and courtesy is no less deserving for anyone. I believe that respect should be mutual not just given to those who appear to have more maturity, knowledge, hierarchy or power. Respect also means that whilst you might not always agree with the other parties views you can choose to allow those views to be, without being disrespectful. Here is how I believe we can tune into respect more and honor it within our relationships.

- **Value both yours and the other persons needs and feelings** - As said above, you don't need to believe or even understand another person's point of view to show that you value what they are saying and how they are feeling. Showing empathy toward another is a great way of practicing this.
- **Compromising** - Often in relationships, particularly intimate partner relationships, there is an element of compromise that is necessary. When you put any two people together that have grown up with different 'rules' of how the world should work it can be challenging. If you can practice empathy and be flexible in situations, then the skill of both parties compromising to reach an amicable solution that honors each other's core needs, works a treat.
- **Boundaries** – We set them, and we are given them! Honor the other person's boundaries and hold your own boundaries. Acknowledging and respecting someone else's boundaries is just as key as keeping your own boundaries in place.
- **Speak kindly** – This is relevant when speaking to a person directly and behind their back. There is no quicker way to lose respect than to be found gossiping about someone behind their back, or partaking in conversation that attunes to this behaviour without stepping away. Have integrity for yourself and respect the person enough to speak only with kindness. As the old saying goes "*if you don't have anything nice to say then say nothing at all*".

- **Treat the other person as whole** - When you can see that everyone is complete and there is nothing you need to do to improve or change them, you can begin to fully respect and learn to appreciate truly who they are.
- **Practice self-respect** - Self-respect can be described as accepting yourself fully, all of you! Honouring your voice, emotions, needs and opinions. You are valid, you matter and remember that you are always doing the very best you can in every situation.

All Emotions Are Valid

Something we get taught from a young age is which emotions are ok for us to feel and express and which emotions are not ok to feel and express. We are taught that by merely the reactions people have around us when we feel certain emotions. We say things such as "*don't cry*", we "*shhhh*" people and our intention behind these responses is often that we love them, and we don't want to see them upset. However, as a message in our early years it creates a trigger within us that reminds us about our discomfort with certain emotions when we are an adult. Let me walk you through how to be with all emotions, for yourself and others.

- **Sit with yourself** - First, learn to sit with all of your emotions, and what I mean by '*sitting*' with your emotions, is that when you feel an emotion rise you do not need to act. You can practice observing it, have no attachment or judgement to it, feel the sadness, happiness, anger etc. within you and let it be present and experienced. Allow the feeling to be observed for as long as you can. Everyone has different thresholds on this, so you will know when it becomes too uncomfortable for you. Think about this practice being a muscle that you are strengthening every time you workout. The benefit to this practice is that over time you will become confident and in control of your emotions and being able to experience them and express them without judgement.

- **Sit with others** - Learning to sit with others in their emotions is not dissimilar to your own practice, however this is made easier when you have sovereignty over you own. A main message here is to think about what you say before you say it. Remember the pause. Instead of saying things such as "*don't be sad*" or "*don't cry*" try to say "*I'm here for you*" or don't say anything and just be present, fully in the moment.
- **Validation** - When someone is going through any type of emotional experience validate their feelings. This is so powerful in any relationship; however, this is not putting labels on the emotions you assume you are witnessing or observing, this is acknowledging that it is ok for feelings and emotions to be expressed. You can do this by saying something like, "*how you are feeling right now is perfectly normal*", "*everyone feels like this at some point*". Notice there is no insertion of an emotion, just a gentle validation that their feelings matter.

Relationships are complex and beautiful, they take work, love and reflection for them to be at their ultimate. The journey might seem rough sometimes, but it is so worth it. The deeper connections you feel, the more you will experience life as a whole. Relationships make our lives whole and complete. I hope that the learnings and lessons that lead to the seven aspects above bring you closer to consciously creating your best relationships. Come back to the lessons from time to time when you feel yourself being challenged.

I love to do a relationship audit every now and then, to acknowledge, appreciate and take ownership of how I am showing up in those relationships, how am I owning my contribution, consciously. It's a necessary practice to be present and considerate and keep awareness that critical factors haven't evolved or moved on that I might need to readjust. Here is my relationship self-check in, a few questions for you to reflect on the relationships in your life and assess their status, so that you maintain alignment with all of the aspects that make for your consciously created, aligned and thriving relationships.

- Are you aware of when you are in your masculine or feminine state?
- When you spend time with people in the relationships you have chosen, do you feel energised?
- When you spend time with people in the relationships you have chosen, do you feel drained?
- Do you feel understood by the people around you?
- Do you feel fully able to be yourself around others?
- Do you know your boundaries in your relationships?

- Do you feel that you are able to communicate your boundaries with others?
- Do you feel that these boundaries get respected?
- Do you feel that you are able to identify, manage and express your emotions effectively?
- Are you able to actively listen to others without thinking about what you will say next?
- Are you able to sit in the moment and be present with yourself?
- Do you feel heard by others?

Once you have completed your audit you can take constructive action to rectify anything that feels out of alignment for you. This will enable you to remain on top of your relationships and keep Consciously Connected to one of the healthiest and most important parts of this gorgeous human experience.

ABOUT BECK THOMPSON

Beck Thompson is a Relationship Coach and the owner and founder of The Relationship Circle - a no BS relationship coaching that digs deep, gets to the truth and supports you in creating new behaviours and patterns that re-energise and revitalise your relationship as well as create resilience – reconnecting strong bonds that make you feel whole again.

She believes that when life throws you relationship curve balls, you need to dig deep, face the true issues and get real strategies that work now. Whether you're in the first-year relationship blues, stumbling through moving into together, getting married, the first few years of having kids, or them leaving home, life's relationship circle can sometimes be rough, and you may need a little help along the way.

Working with individuals or couples she supports you to uncover the real issues and find strategies to reconnect and build relationship resilience. She can help you find your way to a more loving, compassionate relationship that remains true through any of life's storms.

Drawing on over 10 years in counselling, social work and life coaching, Beck's no nonsense, deep approach seeks to understand what's happening for you and your partner now. Beck works with you to identify the issues and change behaviour patterns for each person in a compassionate and loving way which allows you to find your way back to each other. With honesty, openness and support, Beck will help you re-establish strong bonds that can endure life's challenges.

E: hello@therelationshipcircle.com

W: www.therelationshipcircle.com

Work with Beck: https://TheRelationshipCircle.as.me/

facebook.com/therelationshipcircle

instagram.com/the_relationship_circle

“

ENJOY THE WORLD AROUND YOU, IT IS PART OF YOU, AND YOU ARE PART OF IT. TOGETHER WE IMPRINT OURSELVES ON ONE ANOTHER, NEVER TO BE THE SAME AGAIN

CONSCIOUS SOUL SPACE

BY JUDE SMITH

'What you surround yourself with, is as important as who you surround yourself with'.

Now do I have something remarkable to share with you, following on so poignantly from Beck's insights talking about relationships? Yes!!!

The Conscious You is in a relationship with your living space!

Just as you influence your living space, your living space influences you. So, wouldn't it be great then, if that influence was an intentional, conscious, soul replenishing joy?

Ever winced away from the mound of laundry or the dirty dishes? Yeah, me too... How do you think your space feels about that?

I know I always feel much better when the chores are done (even if I don't always enjoy doing them). Everything feels brighter and clearer. Life feels more possible. You feel more connected to *The Conscious You*. And when you clear up all those papers on your desk, doesn't the space feel lighter, brighter and happier?

I'm Jude. I'm a Soul Coach and Land Healer and a lover of beautiful, soulful spaces. I share my living space with my husband, my twin teenage sons, and the cat who chose to live with us instead of the neighbours. My surroundings are all too often full of cat fur and the smell of boy socks, but despite that I have created spaces here that soothe and replenish my soul, and that smell good too!

It has taken me years to figure out the process I am going to share with you. There has been much experimentation and trials, and more than a few errors along the way. I've read more books on interior design and decluttering than my husband can roll his eyes at and I've scrolled through dozens, if not hundreds, of blog posts on minimalism and simple living. I've 'KonMari'd'[1] and 'clutterbusted'[2] and 'S.H.E.D'[3] and decluttered and 'feng shuied'[4] and taken more boot-loads of stuff than I care to remember to charity shops. Yet, despite all that, it wasn't until I began to deal with my inner clutter that my spaces really began to fill with soul. A tidy sock drawer only gets you so far. You need to heal your insides, so your soul can shine in your surroundings.

I'm an interior lover, not a trained interior designer. My formal training was all about being a good student and historian. I imagine you're wondering how I came to this work then? How did I learn to consciously create soul in my home?

Let me take you on a journey, my journey of how I came to understand and work with the energy of the space around me, and how you can too.

I should warn you before we start that this journey of mine is as much about spirituality as it is about living space. These strands are so interwoven in my life that it's impossible to separate them out.

There were clues early in my life that I wasn't going to turn out quite like everyone else. Whether it was me trying to understand the stories the birds sang at sunset or hearing all the voices in the old whare nui[5] at the museum. No matter how hard I tried to be sensible and 'normal' and do things 'properly', it never quite stuck. I seemed to feel things more than others, see and hear differently from others, and pick up on things that others just wandered by. It was something of a relief to learn the word 'eccentric' as an older child and realise that this natural oddness of mine could be something aspirational!

As a teenager, my spiritual gifts started becoming more evident. I began to have occasional visions and hear voices in my head. Fortunately for me, this was taken by my church community of the time as signs of the Holy Spirit at work, so instead of ending up in the psychiatric system, I received basic training in managing the flow of these gifts. This stood me in good stead as my path developed over the years.

I have always been a very visual person, so how my living space looks has always been important to me. I would spend my school holidays rearranging my bedroom, trying to get the most out of that small space, making room for more books and art on the shelves and walls. In my last two years of high school, I discovered the wonderful world of art history, at last, something I could study by looking at pictures! Through that I discovered the power of composition, how the arrangements of things in space can evoke emotions, direct the eye, and create powerful effects.

In 1993, in the final year of my Bachelor's degree, in history and, yes, art history, I discovered the interior design section of the library. All those wonderful books and magazines full of inspiration and helpful tips, and some compelling examples of what not to do! I toyed with the idea of formally studying interior design and making it my career path. My friends talked me out of that, but I continued to read the books and continued to work on making my rented rooms into cosy living spaces. On a student budget, there were limits to what I could achieve, but my ever-growing art print and indoor plant collections definitely helped. And I began to learn to listen for the inner feeling of '*yesness*' when a space is happy.

Then I got married. And two and a half years later, I got divorced. Walking out on my first husband opened my eyes and changed my path in profound ways.

What had enabled me to leave him was realising that the promise made with god in my creation/birth outweighed any promise made between two humans. The only way I could've stayed in that marriage was by destroying myself, and I was sure that I had been created the way I was for reasons that did not include self-destruction.

My light during this dark time were my new housemates in my new home. I was fortunate to have a diverse bunch of friends, some of whom took me in when I left my marriage. A bunch of agnostics and pagans, who together patched me up, found space for me, and responded to my situation in a way I knew the Jesus of the gospels would recognise. Living there, I found my healing and I found new options.

A critical insight that I learnt through that time in my life that I will share with you now, is to always remember that you, too, are created for far more than destroying yourself for another human. You have gifts and skills and a soul this world needs. No one is worth destroying yourself for.

Through my history studies, I discovered Celtic Christianity. As someone of Celtic/Cornish ancestry, I felt drawn to this, not just from my ancestry, which is also tied closely to the Methodism I grew up with, but from an inner resonance. My faith had always been creation focused; nature was my church as much as the buildings I went to on Sunday mornings. And I never quite understood why we needed to be saved from this wonderful world our god had created.

Browsing the web rings (yes, this was back in the days of web rings![6] So last century!) of Celtic Christianity led to me stumbling over Celtic paganism. At first, I was so caught in my old paradigm of the Christian god being the only truth that I ran away from these sites. Over the weeks, I began to read and ponder these new-to-me concepts and discuss them with my housemates. My paradigm began to shift, and my spiritual world began to open. All this knowledge I was acquiring was leading me towards a bigger destination, one I could never have foreseen, but there was immense power in my curiosity.

Six months into this new chapter of my life and I no longer called myself Christian. I wasn't yet sure what I was, but I knew my theology had changed in deep ways. Another six months on, and I knew what religious label now fitted me - pagan. (Twenty-mumble years on, that label still fits me, even though my path has developed considerably over the years.)

It was during this time that my housemates and I realised our home was haunted.

The haunting was focused around the back porch. Which was rather inconvenient as this was right beside the fridge in our kitchen, and you had to go through the back porch to reach the laundry. We all started doing our laundry by daylight only, and late night snacking dropped right away. The shadowy presence you could almost see, and most certainly feel, through the textured back door glass grew stronger. We started to hear footsteps in the wooden hallway when no one was there. And visitors started getting spooked about the back door, too. Eventually, we decided something had to be done. But what?

One of my housemates had some experience with energy work. She offered to anchor me and feed me energy, while I tried to make contact with our haunt. I'm still not sure why I was the one who ended up leading the charge. But, as it turned out, I had the right sort of gifts for the job.

We made our attempt in daylight. Sitting in the lounge, trying to not look over to the porch, I put myself into a light trance and reached out with my spirit...

"*MOOOOOOOO!!!*" I was straight back in my body with the sound echoing through my head.

"*It's a cow*" I said.

Yes, our dark presence was the ghost of a cow. Really.

I went back into a trance and reached out again. The cow ghost was distraught. She was separated from her calf and couldn't find it. I went in deeper. I saw a vision of someone murdering her calf, back in the time when our suburb was farmland. And I saw our cow starving herself to death waiting for her calf to return.

I still don't know how, but somehow I managed to call the spirit of her calf to her. And I watched the two of them reunite and walk off and disappear.

When I came out of the trance, there was no trace of that dark presence. We had no further problems or weirdness. I had done my first land healing.

This was just the beginning of my spiritual adventures. Over the next few years, I trained in shamanic techniques of spirit journeying and trance work, learning to work with energy, learning to work with spirits and the unseen world. And my network of invisible spirit friends grew alongside my network of visible human friends and I even got married again.

In 2003, my new husband and I shifted to a house by a river.

We loved the sprawling house and garden, with the river running through the back of the property. Though there was that one spot on the back path that I avoided after dark. We moved in and began to make it our own: repainting, replanting and rearranging. Then, without really meaning to, I became pregnant. I had never particularly wanted to have kids. I wasn't entirely opposed to the idea. But it wasn't something I craved or sought. My childhood dreams were not of being a mum or grandmother. No, I wanted to be eccentric Great Aunt Judith, wearing tweed and comfy boots and with a mysterious handbag full of amazingness! Babies were messy, noisy things and not really that cute. The '*Powers That Be*' had other ideas...

Nine months later, my twin sons were born. And, one day when they were having their afternoon sleep, I finally plucked up the courage to explore the energy of the weird cold spot on the back path that I hated walking through after dark. I spirit journeyed to my back yard, and found myself slipping back a few centuries to when this place was a swampy wetland, not a suburban street... And I watched a tragic event unfold. After healing the energetic and spiritual effects of that event, I never felt the weird coldness there again.

In 2008, on my lads' fourth birthday, we moved into our current home. We fell in love with the light and the space here, up on a hill with expansive views to the surrounding hills, and a forest reserve just up the road. As the only woman in the household (even our then cat was a boy), I quickly staked my claim to a large room to be my craft studio, dance space, and spiritual work space. This space was, and still is, mine, all mine!

Another insight for the record, I definitely agree with Virginia Woolf about every woman needing a room of her own. I think every person, whatever their gender, should have a space to call their own. To thrive as humans, we benefit from having a space we can have complete creative control over and can mould to our needs and wishes.

My dream for my space, was for a spacious expanse within which I could unleash all my creativity and spirituality.

My reality was a cluttered mess filled to the brim and beyond with half-finished projects, potential future projects, stuff that might be useful one day, and a whole bunch of random things I didn't even know if I liked, and my altar jammed up in a corner. The ideas, possibilities, and emotions piled up around me. I literally had a dozen creative projects on the go at any one time, plus I had my job and my family life, and I couldn't figure out why I felt so swamped, overwhelmed and depressed.

At first, I tried dealing with the physical stuff, getting rid of the tired grey geometric wallpaper and painting my room a beautiful leaf green. I set things up the way I had in the past, shelves on the wall, baskets of yarn, boxes of fabric, art where I could fit it in... It helped a little, but not enough. I was still swamped.

I made attempts at decluttering and using the things I had, but there was still far more to process and deal with. Looking back now, I can see how much my inner clutter held me back and contributed to my outer clutter, so many emotions tied up in my stuff, and I couldn't figure out how to process the stuff, physically or emotionally.

It was 2013 when I finally realised what my '*problem*' was.

There was something in my way – ME!

Yes, I was healing bits of me here and there, but I was still buried in layers of childhood learning and pain, and beliefs about what other people expected of me. What I wanted for me was in there somewhere, as were my hopes, my dreams, and my soul. I couldn't see these clearly through all my outer and inner clutter.

Throughout this time, my spiritual practice was my refuge, the place where I could be most me. I became increasingly aware of a growing disconnect between my spiritual life and the reality of my everyday life. And I grew increasingly ready for this to change.

I longed to connect to myself deeply, body, mind, soul and life all flowing together.

In one moment late in 2013, I saw my blocks clearly. And I remembered a possible pathway forward, Julia Cameron's book '*The Artist's Way*'[7].

'*The Artist's Way*' is a 12-week programme of guided journaling to heal your creative life. I had heard of it, borrowed it from the library, and played around its edges, but I hadn't previously committed to doing the work.

I bought my own copy and consciously chose to dig in.

The daily journaling practices that book taught has been immensely powerful for me. It has helped me face my past and begin to heal it. To open my eyes and see the beliefs and conditionings I was carrying that weren't helping me, and I began to consciously change these. To start to dream of a different life, and to actually create it. I still journal most days. It is the practice that helps me be most myself, as writing by hand always shakes loose what's bothering me and helps me find my way forward. Any time I feel stuck, I pull out paper and pen. And every time it works to get me moving again.

As I healed and shed my inner clutter, I began to release more and more of my outer clutter and all the emotions buried within it. At times, I have felt like an infinitely-layered onion, being peeled away piece by piece with always another layer to go. Each layer peeled away has brought me closer to my soul and my truth. Other people's truths and ideas that I once carried as my own have fallen away and my own soul now shines more brightly. And my spiritual path has grown along with me.

Just like in the rest of my life, I've shifted from trying to do things '*properly*' by other people's standards to understanding how to do things the way that works for me. I moved away from group rituals and formal celebrations, and all the expectations and ideas about '*proper ways of doing things*' that I once held. I now celebrate the turn of the year quietly as I work in my own garden. And I no longer feel I have anything to prove. I don't have to look or act a certain way to be a '*proper*' pagan or a '*proper*' anything!

This has been quite a recent development. And I blame this shift primarily on the prodding of my goddess, Bast, the ancient Egyptian cat goddess of love and beauty. She invited me to be her priestess a few years ago, and I accepted. I have realised since that she and her feline children have been a constant spiritual presence throughout my life, and in past lives, too.

I had all kinds of ideas about what a priestess should do. Surely, I should be doing regular prayers and offerings, leading rituals, serving a human community? She said "*no*". She didn't want my service or fancy rituals or anything like that. Yes, I could have an altar to her, and I could be kind to cats, but that was it. Surely, I should be serving my goddess? She said again, very firmly "*No*". This left me baffled and bewildered. How could I call myself a '*proper*' priestess if I wasn't doing anything priestessy?! All She would say is "*you ARE my priestess*". Eventually I realised that it wasn't the doings and the trappings and the looking right that mattered. Yes, I *could* do all sorts of priestessy things. But that wasn't what my goddess wanted. She wanted me to BE me.

One of the ways I honour my goddess is by doing what I can to bring more love and beauty into the world. Creating soul space is a part of this, and it is an important spiritual practice for me. Yet, embracing my own beauty has been a challenge for me. While I enjoy creating and being in beautiful surroundings, and this work comes very naturally to me, I never considered myself to be beautiful. Walking with Bast has helped me begin to appreciate myself more, and to begin to appreciate that I do have my own beauty, even if I'm not '*properly*' beautiful in a conventional way. Learning to love my own eccentric beauty helps me see and love the eccentric beauty in other people and spaces.

This spiritual journey of discovery has helped me figure out more about who I am and what I want this life to be. Yet, despite all this growth and healing, I still felt a sense of disconnect between my space and me. All I was learning and doing was helping, but it hadn't got me all the way to truly en*joy*ing my space.

Then, just this year, I figured out what was missing.

The key piece of the puzzle, which had been sitting there all along unnoticed and unused, was in my spirituality. And, in particular, working with the energy of a space and the spirit of that space.

As someone who works with land spirits to do my land healing, and who understands that there is a spiritual element to all places, this was more of a '*derp*' moment for me than an '*a-ha*'! How had I missed this for so long?

I don't know. I really don't know why it took me so long to put the pieces together. What's more important is that I have now figured it out! And it was my land healing work that gave me the clue.

As I carried out land healings around the world from the comfort of my couch (hurrah for spirit journeying, it's much cheaper and comfier than flying, and there's no jet lag!), I found myself wondering how we could all care more for our land and our spaces, so that less land healing is needed in the future. That got me thinking about how we interact with our surroundings, and how our surroundings interact with us. There is definitely a relationship there.

What might be possible then, if we could get the energy of our living space flowing harmoniously with our own energy?

And there it was! My missing piece, working with the energy and the spirit of my space, not just with myself and my clutter.

There is more to my space than just me. My space has its own ideas about what it wants and needs. It has its own history and energy layered up onion-like, just like me. And just like me, it sometimes needs some healing, too. Working together with my space has enabled me to get past my disconnection and finally, finally, FINALLY create spaces that aren't just decluttered, but that sing deeply to my soul. Now my living space replenishes me. Now I sit down at my desk with joy – because it is a soul space for me. Now I can truly not only live but thrive in my living space!

And because I've worked it out, you can do this for yourself, and your soul too.

Creating soul space is all about consciously creating a loving connection with your living space. Your living space is quite literally the space where you live so it should enliven you. When we feel a loving connection with our living and working spaces, it supports us to thrive.

Creating soul space with love and intention strengthens the energy exchange between ourselves and our living space in a hugely positive way. Energy exchange between ourselves and our space will happen whatever the quality of our connection to our surroundings, just as Samantha taught us, so we might as well create a positive exchange.

Creating soul space for myself has taken my living spaces to the next level, replenishing my energy and making me smile even when I'm sitting down to work or cleaning up! My soul spaces make my life easier and better, and deeper and more purposeful. Consciously creating soul space enables me to flow with clarity and intention into consciously creating the rest of my life.

I've also seen the power of soul space in my client's lives. I love watching the transformation from tired space to soul space, that never gets old. Watching people create spaces that allow them to truly thrive brings me to tears of joy and awe. It feels such an honour to hold space for this work.

I look back now on old photos of my studio in cluttered mess mode and I feel nauseous when I see all the stuff piled up around the room and across the floor. I am so grateful I found a way to finally get to the spacious and creative room I dreamed of, the expansive, soul-filled space I am writing this chapter in! I sit here typing with tonnes of room to stretch and breathe around me, my orchid and cyclamen sitting on my desk beside me, with my music playing softly, and my cat snoozing in the sun. Such a joy, this soul space of mine.

And I want this for you, too. That's why I'm writing this, why I'm sharing my story, why I do this work. I want you to live with joy, to thrive in your soul space! To be sure, your soul space probably won't look anything like mine or anyone else's soul space. And, you know what? That's wonderful! Your soul isn't the same as mine or anyone else's either so, why would your space look the same? Your soul space will work for your soul and your life. That's as it should be.

And the best thing about it all is that, while my journey has taken me years, you can jump in right now and use what I've learned straight away.

So, let's get to it! Let's get you creating your soul space.

Choose your space

Consciously choose your space, to begin:

- start with a small space
- start with a space you see every day
- start with a space you have complete creative control over

Some spaces that are good places to start - your bedside table and surrounds, the surface of your desk, a shelf or shelving unit that is yours alone...

Why start small? Well:

- A small space is achievable in a short time.
- A small visible space is something you can enjoy every day.
- A small visible space you have complete creative control over is a space the rest of your household shouldn't be dumping their papers or dirty coffee mugs in the midst of it (and you can set some clear boundaries if they do, go back to Becks chapter for

that gold!)

You can '*soul*' other spaces, like your drawers and cupboards and living room, later on. These will be easier if you've created some soul space for yourself already.

Remember to take a '*Before*' photo of your chosen space.

Assess your space

Grab your notebook and sit in or beside your chosen space. Answer these questions:

- What works for you in the space as it is?
- What isn't working for you?
- What do you love about this space?
- What do you need to use this space for?
- How does this space really feel to you?

This will bring you greater clarity on what you are feeling from the energy of the space currently, and in your envisaged future.

Chat with your space

Sit in or beside your space and ask it what it wants.

Write down any ideas or thoughts that arise, no matter what they might be.

Now ask your space how you can work together to create this.

Allow this information to come through you, receive everything with kindness and curiosity, release all judgements and connection to a particular outcome.

Set your intention

Drawing on your notes, write a list of words that describe how you want this space to be and feel. Aim for about twenty words.

Now review your list and highlight the ones that call to you most, the words that really capture how you want your space to be and how you want to feel in this space. Note down any other words that spring to mind as you do this.

Keep reviewing until you have a list of two to five keywords for your space. These are your intentions for this space. If you like you can make these into a sentence: "*My (space) feels ____, ____ and _____*".

This brings greater meaning and clarity to what you are going to achieve through souling your space, and helps you call forth everything that brings with it the energy of those key words.

Clearing and cleaning

Now we get physical!!!

Clear everything out and off your space and clean the space thoroughly.

I recommend cleaning/dusting everything as you take it out. Find a safe place to put things, even if it's just alongside. Yes, it will look messier for a bit. That's okay, it's only temporary.

As you clear, you may find things that you no longer need or want any more so recycle, donate, or bin these as appropriate.

When you're done, you may like to refresh the energy of your space by:

- opening a window or two and letting the air blow through
- ringing a bell or clapping your hands around the space (remember the corners)
- burning incense or a smudge stick or a candle in the space
- turning the music up and dancing in or around your space

Pause for a moment and notice the feel of your space now. How has this shifted?

Create and curate

This is my favourite step!

Now you get to put things back in!!

Grab your intentions and keep these somewhere visible while you create your space.

Look at the things you cleared out, do each of these fit your intentions? Feel into this, how do you want this space to feel? Will this '*thing*' help, does it meet your intentions?

If it's a "*No*", you're going to find a new home for them (whether in your home or beyond). Remove these things from the space you're focusing on now and put them somewhere they can wait until you do find their homes.

If it's a "*Yes*", try putting them in your space. Does that truly feel like your intention? Be really honest. If not, remove them as above.

Play with placing your "*Yes*" things in your space and arranging them all so the space feels good and meets its function. Do this until it suits you and suits your intention. It's your space, so let your style and aesthetics rampage freely! *Do You!*

Are there things that you need for this space? Do you have anything suitable anywhere else in your house? Bring that in (with a quick clean), remembering your intention. If you don't have anything suitable, make a shopping list.

When you're done, pause for a few minutes and enjoy your space. Notice how it feels. Smile at your space and appreciate it. Tweak it a little more if it needs it, then enjoy it some more.

Dedicate and enjoy

This step helps you deeply connect with your freshly souled space and enjoy it all the more.

To dedicate your space, do one or more of these (adjusting to suit your space):

- light a candle in your space and watch it burn, feeling that fiery energy charge the space.
- breathe deeply and slowly, letting the air from your lungs fill the space.

- hold a cup of water in your hands and send loving energy to it, flick this water around the space or sit in the space and sip the water slowly.
- place your hands palm down on the surface of your space, close your eyes and feel the texture of the surface, feel where your hands meet the space, feel the energy that flows between you and your space.

Sit in your space and enjoy it. Use it as you intended.

Jot down in your notebooks your impressions of your space now:

- What do you love about this space?
- How does it feel to be in it and use it?
- Are there still things you want to change about it? Can you change that now? (You have permission!)

Take another photo of your space, so you have a record of your "*after*" to go with your "*before*". I'd love to celebrate your soul space journey with you. Send me your before and after photos, so I can cheer you on!

Enjoy the soul space you have created. Look after it, clean it regularly, refresh its energy as needed, adjust and change it as needed. You can continue to practise the steps above; this is not a one-time only practise. You are going to grow and change, let your space come on that journey with you. You may find a regular review of the space is helpful, so that you keep pace with each other, you could do this each season or each year or whenever the urge strikes.

Once you have one space souled, choose another to '*soul*', work through the prompts, set your intentions, make your changes. You can '*soul*' as much of your living space as you like. You can also take it outside your home, see how much soul you can bring into your work space. And, if you want to get really bold and souled, you can even apply this process to things like your hobbies and your schedule...

When you get to the communal areas of your home, it is both polite and loving to involve the other members of your household who also use the space. Run through the prompts together and get them to help with the cleaning too. Set your intentions for the space together and have fun arranging things together.

Souling your space, is like caring for another aspect of yourself. As I said at the beginning it is a relationship that we have with our environment. We are connected because of the space we co-inhabit. We cannot be separate, and we need to communicate. *The Conscious You* knows the power in this practise, and when you have gone through this process, your soul source energy will feel it too.

ABOUT JUDE SMITH

Jude Smith is a Soul Coach and Land Healer.

Jude's first adventures with land healing came from living in a house haunted by the ghost of a cow (yes, really). She has spent the twenty plus years since then developing her spiritual gifts and diving deep into the world of energy and spirit. In 2016, she left her office job and devoted herself to soul coaching and land healing fulltime.

As a Soul Coach, she supports the soul journey of her clients through one-to-one coaching, group programmes, and courses.

As a Land Healer, she works long distance around the world to heal energetic and spiritual issues with people's homes and neighbourhoods.

A priestess of Bast (the ancient Egyptian cat goddess of love and beauty), Jude is passionate about appreciating the beauty around us and within us, and about healing this planet and its inhabitants (whatever their species) from a space of love. She is also an advocate for sustainable spirituality: spiritual practices which sustain us, which we can sustain, and which don't wreck the planet.

Jude lives in Wellington, New Zealand with her husband, twin teenage sons, the cat formerly known as the neighbours, and her ever-growing collection of indoor plants.

E: jude@thejudesmith.com

W: www.thejudesmith.com

 facebook.com/thejudesmith

 instagram.com/thejudesmith

"

BARRIERS COME IN ALL SHAPES AND SIZES TO TEACH, TEST AND SHOW US OUR OWN POSSIBILITIES. HOW YOU CHOOSE TO SEE THEM IS A CONSCIOUS CHOICE

CONSCIOUSLY CONTROLLING ANXIETY

BY LEESA WATT

'Imagine a light, highly functioning soul energy shocked into vibrating and processing a lower frequency in an earthly dimension – that's anxiety!'

Yes, I see you anxiety, but you will not win today!! Can I just say if you have anxiety, you are not weird. It's just that our flight and fight responses are extreme. Everybody has this, ours is just off the charts, which makes us kind of special.

My name is Leesa and I suffer with anxiety, I know the struggles and I am here to help those suffering or feeling limited with their anxiety, and teach them that life isn't over, you can consciously create your best life and it can be everything you want it to be and more. *The Conscious You* can have anxiety and still handle life like a boss – let me show you what I mean...

I was born strong, determined, an empathic introvert. I was laid back, easy going, just living one day to the next. I never really knew what I wanted to be when I grew up. It became apparent as I got closer to forty that I didn't just want to exist and live day to day. I want to lay there at the end of my life and say, '*I did that, I made a difference, go me!*'

Over the past twelve years I have grown, going through a fair share of personal turmoil and stress. You know things like, raising children, divorce, selling a family home, business failures, moving, living on welfare. Some days I was fine and then other days I just couldn't '*life*'. I'd lay in bed, I'd cry uncontrollably, I couldn't make a decision to save myself.

Let me tell you a story about '*Mrs. Perfect*', my life and how it used to look, I had everything. A son and daughter in a happy marriage, with a healthy bank account, a lovely house, holidays and adventures, lots of friends, plenty of laughs, a million good times and lots and lots of love.

But, along came anxiety and everything about me and what I thought had been my '*Perfect life*' changed. I was frozen, trapped and so very scared, not being able to get out of bed for days on end.

I had experienced a few weird episodes before I visited the doctor and even questioned whether it was menopause or perhaps a stroke. I experienced hot flushes, diarrhoea, trembling, numbness, a pounding heart. I was afraid to leave the house and was mapping out exit strategies for every situation. I knew where every public toilet was and I was crying, all the time, so many tears. I'd never felt so alone, so strange and I just wanted to sleep to avoid it all. This is how my anxiety presented and it came out of the blue without warning and without any way for me to determine what was happening. I had no idea this was anxiety, it felt like a nightmare.

My first 'episode' occurred when I had taken my son for private swimming lessons along with a determined toddler. As soon as we had arrived at the pool I felt a hot flush rising that I couldn't control, and I spent the entire lesson in the swimming instructor's bathroom pouring water over myself. I felt like I was on fire. I could barely stand, and I wasn't sure if I needed the toilet or felt nauseous. I remember thinking "*please not now, how embarrassing and get me out of here*". I'm sure the instructor thought I was insane and kept on asking if I was safe to drive. I couldn't get home fast enough and had to lay under the air con before I got the kids in the car to travel the two and a half hours to my parents' house. On my first attempt, I made it half an hour up the road before I turned around and came back home for fear I'd need a toilet. I also hate using public toilets and was stressed how I'd deal with two kids '*if*' I needed to go. I sat in my car until I calmed down and then started to drive it was exhausting. I finally arrived and walked into my parent's hours later and went straight to bed.

Then there was an outing to the theatre with just mum and me for her birthday. We'd got dressed up, had the best seats and were so excited for a girls' day out. We got there and I remember feeling a wave of nerves wash over me, I looked for the closest toilet, which had a line a mile long. Mind you I didn't need to go. I was merely looking for that elusive safe space where there could be no eyes on me. This unrecognisable fear raced through my body. My heart was pounding, my stomach doing cartwheels. I mentioned to mum that I suddenly didn't feel so good, but I thought once we were seated I'd be fine.

The next problem I encountered was that we were in the middle of the row, so immediately my mind was racing ahead to plan my exit strategy, how was I going to get out of here in a hurry and, would that toilet line still be long? I tried to pull myself together, but my mind wouldn't stop racing. I just wanted to be at home, in my bed. Sitting in our row, confined in the middle, I lightly tapped mum's arm and said that I really didn't feel good. She told me to "*see how you go*". The show started and I couldn't focus, all these feelings were still there. I told mum I couldn't do it, I couldn't stay, but I didn't want her to miss out. Of course, she didn't want me to go alone but I managed to convince her to stay and enjoy herself, I didn't want to ruin her experience. I took her car and drove myself home wondering the whole way, what on earth was happening to me. I got home and cried to my then husband that something wasn't right. This was one of the first of Leesa's fleeing sprees.

That weekend I was wiped out and spent most of my time in bed. My symptoms were all still there, the racing heart, tingling hands and lips. They'd come and go in waves. My mum was the only '*calm*' influence and I needed her to just lay with me, quietly. At one point, I could hear my family discussing how they'd get me to go and see a doctor. Saying they might need to call an ambulance to hospitalise me. I remember thinking to myself maybe I do need a rest, time to sleep, no mothering duties...oh a lovely hospital vacation. Where in fact my family were meaning, I might need to visit a psych ward. The panic button was pushed!!! I finally agreed to a home doctor visit who I still remember said to me, "*if you can't get up for yourself, do it for your kids*".

As soon as I could, I got to my GP with mum by my side. I even couldn't sit and wait for the doctor in the waiting room, so the staff put me in a room to lie down with a Hydralyte to focus on sucking. I honestly thought I was going to die. The doctor knew what was wrong straight away, "*you have anxiety*" she said. "*I have what, now?*" And she continued, "*You'll need counselling and meds*". "*Drugs, you're drugging me?*" I was catatonic, and you can only imagine how my anxiety was presenting!

She asked me '*if I had high blood pressure would I take a tablet to improve it and my health?*' Naturally I said, "*hell yes!*" So why was I baulking at taking something to make my life better?

The doctor said I could go on a mental health plan. "*Excuse me, I'm mental now?*"

I felt ashamed, like a failure. Visions of white strait jackets haunted me. I couldn't make sense of it. I had a loving family, I wanted for nothing. I couldn't believe this was happening. I felt judged. I felt like I'd lost it. I kept thinking, '*I am strong, I am funny, and I don't have a care in the world*'. I remember calling and telling friends what was happening with me, no one would believe that I had anxiety.... "*You, Leesa? No way!!!*"

I believe that it was because of how society portrayed '*mental*' at that time that I just couldn't come to terms with it. Thinking of anxiety as a mental illness, to me equated to needing to be locked away in a padded cell. I'd never be normal, kind of like 'One Flew Over The Cuckoo's Nest'[1]. Every time I'd hear the words 'mental health' in a sentence about me I'd shudder. Labels can be mean. Why as a society, are we so judgmental? When I was first diagnosed, anxiety was hardly spoken about, I had to be careful who I told, that I had it. No wonder people are left to suffer in silence. Some friends fell away, they didn't understand, ignorance is easier than empathy, I guess. Is it any wonder we fear being labelled with a mental illness! Being referred to as mad, crazy, unstable. Mental health doesn't detract from who we are.

My family organised to look after the kids while I started the journey with the medication to rebalance the chemicals in my brain. It was the first time that my daughter had stayed away from me since she was born. It was so hard to do, but I knew it was a necessity. It took some time for the medication to kick in and in the beginning, it made my symptoms worse. I met up with the family and my kids for the Easter holidays and I couldn't even leave the apartment. No one really understood what was happening, least of all me. On the outside I was fine, on the inside I was crumbling, compounded by mother's guilt. It was horrific, so I tried something new, I made up a mantra, '*It's a new day*'. I would say it religiously to myself as each day I had no idea what would be thrown at me, but I got up and I showed up as best as I could.

Before I was diagnosed with anxiety, I was super organised and pretty much had a show home, you know shiny kettle that sparkles and all that, always striving for what I thought was perfection. I thought that maybe that expectation of a perpetually clean home was what stressed me out and so I let it go. I ran the house and finances and my husband struggled to pick up the slack. Finding a happy balance ever since has been a struggle. I'll sort things in piles around the house, I'll be overwhelmed to finish a project. I hate deadlines. I hate the phone. I still question the balance all these years later, but I've learnt to live with what I can do and make the best of that. My first outsource for my business was a cleaner, which has been life changing!

I quickly clung to those I trusted, and couldn't cope when people I knew and trusted moved on, like my doctor who left. I became dependent for the first time in my life. I rarely wanted to leave the house just in case I had an attack, the mere thought used to bring one on.

As time went by, I started to panic about panicking. On numerous occasions, I would ring my husband to come home as I couldn't care for the kids. It got to the point where we had to hire a nanny to help me. I had to enrol my daughter in day-care earlier than I would have liked, even though I was at home during the day. I felt useless and experienced mother guilt on an extreme level. I wasn't good enough, or so I thought. I would read technical or medical books and articles about anxiety and the same night I'd have a bloody panic attack about it. I still need to write that comical book on how to deal with being told you have anxiety! You know something like, 'Anxiety for Dummies'.

I began searching for my people, those I could talk to without judgement! I made friends with mums who were experiencing anxiety and we formed a chat group called '*The Nutbags*'. We were always there for each other, sharing our stories, our fixes. That support was invaluable, and their friendship is still there today. When I was experiencing panic attacks or anxiety I would text to distract myself, my poor mum and sisters would have texts at all times of the day and night and reply by talking me through it. It's funny how the best of plans can be forgotten when anxiety really kicks in, when it was really bad I couldn't even use the phone and would forget to use my '*toolbox*', of recovery and aid ideas and strategies, until someone would say, "*have you tried your oils today?*" My closest friends would drop everything to come watch my kids while I rode the roller coaster. Then I'd cry that I was ruining my kid's life, I wasn't a good enough mother. I am so grateful for all the support I received back then; I don't know where I would have been without it.

One of my first huge lessons in coming to terms with my anxiety and learning to take control, was learning to say "*No*", with no guilt, overwhelm and no attachment. In my former persona as '*Mrs. Perfect*' I'd always offer to do everything for everyone no matter what was already on my plate, I felt so guilty if I said no. Yet I struggled to ask for help, still to this day I find it hard to let someone help me, but I still use the word "*No!*"

I didn't click with my first counsellor, looking back I don't think I wanted to accept that I had anxiety and needed help. There was one lesson I took from her though, the metaphor of when a plane goes through a cloud and it comes out the other side. She reminded me anxiety was silent and that no one knew I was experiencing it, "*remember Leesa it will stop*", she would say. I found a new counsellor and cried a thousand tears. She took the time to explain to me that all kinds of people have anxiety, nurses, firemen, doctors etc. I believe there was also something said about anxiety sufferers being highly intelligent (now, I don't mind if you say that). She made me realise that I was no less of a human. I Googled it one day, just to check, and you'd be surprised how many celebrities have anxiety, that's right people you wouldn't expect to! I went to counselling for a good two years, it gave me techniques to deal with what I was experiencing, it gave me confidence and reassurance.

It did take me a while to feel like myself again. I then faced the question of whether to have a third child or not. It meant that I'd have to stop taking my medication and that was a scary prospect, wondering if the attacks would return. I made it through the pregnancy but when it came to the end, I became very nervous to have the actual baby and I was placed on Valium the week before she was due. Only after I asked the obstetrician 100 questions and was reassured that it was safe. As a new mum, for the third time, I soon became very tired and hit a wall, hello anxiety again. Thankfully, I was more prepared this time and knew what I was in for.... grab the '*toolbox*'.

It was just before my daughter's first birthday when my husband told me he wanted to separate. To me this came from nowhere, so unexpected, I dropped to the floor, I couldn't read his five-page letter. We did try to work things out, but he had already '*signed out*'. He moved out two months later. I'm not blaming my anxiety although it was a big part of my marriage ending. I pulled myself together and I found my inner strength. I had my support team and I raised those three kids as a sole parent. I'm not saying it was easy, I'm not saying the anxiety didn't pop up. I did it and I don't think those kids turned out too bad.

Exciting adventures set my anxiety off just as much as stressful ones. Ever since I was a little girl I loved the cinema. My nan took me to see Grease when I was five. Anxiety tried to rob me of the things I loved to do. There were many times sitting in a cinema, excited to see the latest movie and my anxiety would hit, I felt claustrophobic, trapped and the familiar panic would set in. Once I had to sit outside the cinema, where people were walking in to another one, some staring, some stopping to ask if I was okay. The staff brought me water and arranged a refund. As soon as my legs worked, I ran, so embarrassed. But I kept returning to try and defeat my anxiety, I needed to show it who was boss. Slowly the urge to flee subsided and my fight would kick in, it was an exhausting cycle but a necessity to get through to the other side. Just like that plane and the cloud, I started to remember there would be a calm after the storm. The first 'fight' I made myself sit through the movie, shaking. It's like I had to retrain my brain that the cinemas weren't a threat. Finally, I can go and enjoy the movies again, sometimes the nerves are there, but the movies are far too good to not go to.

Fight the anxiety. It can make you or break you. Show up and show anxiety who's boss! Take care of you first, say "*No*", don't overcommit. Plan your time for work, rest and play.

Anxiety is an ongoing journey, you can't switch it on and off as you please, so get your toolbox and tackle it.

I would avoid scenarios that could set off my anxiety, if I had an attack I'd run. Even if that meant packing up at 1am and driving home, yes, I did that a few times. There was a holiday that I went on to the Sunshine Coast in Queensland to reconnect with an old family friend. The kids were excited, it was going to be an adventure. We had a fun filled day, swimming, takeaway for dinner and a few drinks. I felt exhausted and decided to take the kids back to my room. As I lay in bed, my old friend anxiety knocked. "Uh oh here we go". Perhaps a shower would help, nope too late. I was spiralling, I called my partner to see if speaking to him would calm me down. In the middle of our conversation I projectile vomited all over the unit. That was it, I wanted my home! So, after cleaning up, I packed the kids up and drove the hour and a bit back home in the wee hours of the morning. Once I was home, I felt safe, embarrassed but safe.

There was another time when we were staying on the Gold Coast with relatives to watch my nephews footy match. I think I'd had one drink that night. Again, I went to bed with the kids and lay there with a wave of panic settling over me. This time I got up and tried to walk it off. My aunty was about to head to bed but stayed up to help me, and yes that made me feel guilty. I couldn't get the feeling to pass so again I packed the kids up in the middle of the night and made the drive back home. And yes, that's right, once I was home, I was fine.

One family Christmas we were staying in Toowoomba, in

Australia. We'd had a great day, amazing dinner, just a few drinks. There was a little bit of conflict between family members for whatever reason, and as I lay in the lounge the anxiety wave swallowed me whole. My partner and I went outside for a chat. This time I really wanted to stay, all the people I loved were around me. In that moment anxiety decided otherwise. You know the drill, pack the kids up and drive the two hours home, to be completely fine once I was there. I was really starting to become annoyed at anxiety making me run, Leesa's fleeing sprees were becoming all too regular.

With each occasion, I would try to pull it together and over time I became stronger and achieved the win. I was on my way to Sydney with a lady I worked with to attend a baby expo. When we were parking the car, anxiety popped up.... Oh, great timing. I had a vision of calling my partner to come rescue me, and I said "*No*", not today anxiety! I put the boxing gloves on and silently fought. I couldn't eat but I was ok. By the time, we landed in Sydney I was exhausted, and we still had to set a massive display up. Instead of falling apart I celebrated and got on with the job.

Now I've saved the best for last, are you ready for this one? My partner and I had gone on a skiing holiday to New Zealand. On the last night, we met up with his ex-wife who was dating a guy I went to school with (did you get all that? They are now married and yes, we are all friends!), we drank copious amounts of champagne. My partner encouraged me to go to bed just after midnight as we needed to leave at 4am to fly home. I was still drunk! I slept the whole way to the airport. We made it through check in and so on, and then my anxiety hit me. I was a mess, running backwards and forwards to the toilet, shaking almost uncontrollably. My partner was jokingly like "*babe, pull yourself together they won't let you get on the plane you look like a junkie*". The only thing that made me get on that plane was getting home to my babies. I have never felt so sick! I even had to cover my mouth and close my eyes when the meals came out.

So, after these events, I realised that alcohol and anxiety don't mix (for me). I decided to watch when and how much I drank, and things are way better these days. I can still have a celebratory drink and if I'm super comfortable a few glasses of my choosing. Geez it could be worse; a lot of people can't have coffee as it brings on anxiety - now that I wouldn't be comfortable with!

Sometimes we also need to teach others lessons. I was at a Pink concert and had a panic attack. The most exciting time of my life as a VIP ticket holder, out with my sister and friend for a memory making night. We enter the venue and it wasn't even full at that time. We were so close to the stage I started to panic and feel dizzy and claustrophobic (no, this time, I wasn't drunk). I was taken to the first aid room and hung with them for the whole support act. I felt like crap, but I had to see Pink no matter what. The St John's guy said to me, "*why would you buy a ticket to a concert if you have anxiety?*" To which I quickly replied, "*why would I stop living just because I have anxiety?*" It felt so good to stand up for myself! I worked out if I stood near an exit, I felt ok. I trembled that whole concert, but I stayed, and I saw my idol. I now choose better seating and have been to the same venue several times, the nerves are there, but I do ok. Some days it takes the breath out of me and I feel like a truck has hit me. I now know that the next day I wake up stronger, cheering myself on for another achievement!

Anxiety cannot stop me believing in myself, and it shouldn't stop you either.

So, what I am saying is don't give up, listen to your body. Tame the overwhelm, you are good enough, confront your fears, be brave, don't fear the judgement of others, believe in yourself and have all the confidence in the world. Truly, we have the strength within us, and we can deal with whatever is thrown at us. My advice would be to stop suffering in silence, talk to your friends, loved ones, a doctor. Be honest with how you feel, it doesn't make us weak, we are human! Be vulnerable, have the confidence and remember You Are Not Alone.

So, let's talk dating. When do you tell someone about your mental illness? My partner could not be any more supportive. Even when he can't be with me, he's there on the phone helping me. His encouragement has made me feel 'normal'. Let me tell you, for many years I lived in fear he'd run away, especially after what anxiety did to my marriage. He's constantly praising me for how far I've come and how well I manage my anxiety. There are people out there who won't judge your mental health and love you for who you are, you just have to search.

Being a single mum meant I needed an income, yep another stress. It was a dream of mine to open a retail store and the opportunity popped up. I had a very close friend who was keen to be my business partner. After me financing and using my network we opened a children's store. It started well, then we were on different paths for spending etc. and it very quickly turned sour. The business and our relationship ended badly and created more stress (*come on, give me a break, how much stress can one person have in their life?*). I won't go into details, but solicitors were involved, threats were made, and I was locked out. Anxiety, anxiety, anxiety. You'll be happy to know I got back up and I went on my merry way. Money had always provided extra stress. Trying to provide for three kids, being embarrassed when we couldn't afford to go to a play centre with friends, I vowed that it would never happen again, and it hasn't!

I started an online business with the intention of finding a job when my youngest was in prep. I organised pop-up stores, created a wholesale/service business with a friend and that is when I identified that social media was my strong point. It occurred to me that with every job I did I enjoyed more of the marketing side, finally things were clicking into place.

In 2015, I built enough confidence to finally open my very own business. On many occasions I would look at returning to full time work vs having my own business. But who would have the kids before and after school, holidays? It just wasn't feasible or worth it, I'd be left with no money. I stuck with the business and thankfully over the past four years it has grown and supports us all – go me!

Each anxious experience and panic attack has made me stronger. I don't fear it anymore and I am able to push it away before things spiral out of control. It's all in the '*toolbox*'.

So, what's in my toolbox I hear you ask? I use things like essential oils, vision boards, I set goals, I talk about anxiety to whoever will listen, I aim to be as positive as possible, I take time for me and practice lots of self-care, I use lists, I create automations, I rest, I exercise, meditate, I have music playlists, I seek help and most of all I remember to *breathe*!

I feel like I didn't grow up till I turned forty! Being able to make decisions without fearing what others would think or how they'd judge me, was a freedom I hadn't experienced before. It was also when I discovered marketing was meant for me. There weren't too many social media managers when I began and it certainly wasn't considered a job or business, but I knew I had to make it work. I feared the old inner critical voice reminding me that I didn't go to university or have a piece of paper to prove myself. And in all honesty, that one took me awhile to get my head around and quieten the critic. Normally I'd do a job for two years and be bored, looking for the next challenge. Having my own business and one that's not the same every day is a pleasure and I could do it twenty four seven. Don't worry I don't, because that would be bad self-care and no doubt see the return of my anxiety attacks. See, I am learning my anxiety boundaries!

It was only the end of 2018 that I decided it was time for me and took action. I was determined to work on myself, answer all those big questions "*who am I?*" and "*what do I want?*" I met Alison, a Clarity & Success Coach, just what I needed, and set out to see how I could up-level all that I am and have to give, what do I do? I warned everyone in my inner circle that only positive vibes would now surround me, and I got to working on myself.

I'd had a burning desire since 2005 to be involved with, and help people with anxiety. I just couldn't work out how, everything seemed to be volunteer based and as happy as I am to do that, I needed an income first. One of the first things Alison identified was that desire. She saw my eyes light up when I spoke about helping people with anxiety. She suggested including it in my existing business, specifically being there for the anxious entrepreneur. My existing clients we're on board, yup that's right, I was already helping the anxious I just didn't know it. That was a huge "*uh dur*" moment, as well as a huge confirmation that I was on the right track. It's coming up to six months of working with Alison now and I have learnt so much about me. This has *more* than up-levelled my confidence. I've been able to realise how far I've come and been able to celebrate what a successful life I've built for myself and my kids, all whilst helping others even through my anxiety. I now appreciate and own what I have to offer. The reassurance is strong.

Realising I was an introvert at age forty-five (I'm a bit slow) has been mind blowing. I thought I was shy growing up and then at thirty I thought it was all my anxiety. So, I now know I need quiet time, I need recharging, being alone is like medicine, crowds are emotionally draining. Too much peopling! And again, talking to like-minded people has made me not feel so peculiar, given me more tools to manage myself and see all my worth. Knowing and listening to my limits helps me plan how to get through a week, a month, a year.

Being self-employed gives me the versatility I desire to bloom. Each day I can't wait to start work. I haven't sought out clients, they've all come to me via word of mouth because I'm making differences in others' lives, whether it's encouraging, supporting or motivating them, and thus they talk about me and my services. It has been incredible!

By taking care of myself and adapting my lifestyle I've become the happiest I've ever been.

It's amazing what can happen when we put our self-care first. You know what they say, '*You can't pour from an empty cup*'.

I'm not saying Mrs. Perfect is back (nor do I want her to be), but I am saying things are under control and I couldn't be happier with my life. Overwhelm creeps in, but the tools are there and they are used daily to create my best life. Each anxiety attack has built my resilience and courage. By staying one step ahead of my anxiety I've become prepared, ready to fight. Anxiety has taken so many hours of my life away, but it has also taught me so much and made me who I am today.

Here's the good news, *The Conscious You* doesn't have to hide what's so much a part of who you are anymore – it's time to speak up and makes some changes! With all I have experienced and all I have overcome, here are my insights for Consciously Creating a better life when dealing with anxiety:

- See your doctor.
- Do you need medication or perhaps a natural supplement?
- Do you need extra help, counsellors, psychiatrists,

naturopaths, acupuncture etc.? (don't be afraid to get help, you deserve it!)

- Grab your own cheerleaders, those who understand and are there for you 100%!
- Take baby steps to gain control of your life. Gently push yourself to try, maybe that means driving yourself to the destination having a little bit of control makes you more eager and confident.
- Distract yourself, don't let anxiety win.
- As time goes by, push yourself harder and further don't miss out on life at least try, after all what's the worst thing that can happen? Anxiety will occur at some point, and will anyone even notice?
- Make yourself comfortable surround yourself with familiarities. Sit outside at a restaurant where it's cooler and not so crowded, grab a theatre seat at the end of the aisle, map out your exit strategy (it's ok, you probably won't use it), your thoughts are comforted and gives you the courage to go further.
- Exercise to your liking, Meditation, yoga etc.
- Sleep well!
- Watch your own limits and take time out.
- Say "*No*".
- Eat well, does coffee or alcohol make you more anxious?
- Celebrate your wins!
- The most important, talk about it.

My hot tip though is to laugh, always make light of what life throws at you. You've got this!

ABOUT LEESA WATT

Leesa Watt is a single mum to three delightful children. A girlfriend to one amazingly supportive man and one of three daughters to two gorgeous parents. She is an empathic, kind and hilarious social media mentor to entrepreneurs around the world.

Leesa is a dedicated learner in all things business and self-development. She has worked in innovating roles and since having children she unleashed her creativity and worked in her own businesses from retail to wholesale to consulting. Realising at age forty that helping people was where she flourished and needed to be. Leesa has built a portfolio of dream clients and loves her job so much she finds it hard to stop working.

She is particularly passionate about helping people with anxiety and making the world aware.

Born in Sydney Australia she moved to Brisbane as a teen and hasn't looked back. Living a relaxed, chilled life.

Her mission is to help the empathic anxious entrepreneur succeed and show up in their business.

Working with Leesa will give you the tools to balance your overwhelm and shine.

E: social@goldmedia.com.au

W: www.goldmedia.com.au

FG: www.facebook.com/groups/theanxiousentrepreneurs/

L: www.linkedin.com/in/leesawatt/

YT: www.youtube.com/c/GoldmediaAu

AS ONE DOOR CLOSES ANOTHER ONE OPENS, THAT DOESN'T MEAN WE FORGET OR MOVE ON, WE CAN CHERISH, HONOUR AND RESPECT THAT ASPECT OF OURSELVES KNOWING WE CAN MOVE THROUGH DOORWAYS CONFIDENTLY AND COMPASSIONATELY

CONSCIOUSLY RESTARTING

BY CAREY BUCK

'Choosing to begin again takes courage, perseverance and heart, as well as self- love, self-respect and compassion for yourself. It is the understanding that you are the priority now'.

Life doesn't always go according to the plan. Sometimes unexpected and unwanted experiences come to threaten who we are, what we want and need, and we can be plunged into darkness. I believe that we can only be in the darkness for so long, and that we have a duty to ourselves to actively and consciously choose to restart. To actively and consciously choose our conscious self.

I want to tell you of my journey, through my darkest days, and share with you how I found a new life on the other side. It is my intention to explain the insights, tools and practices that enabled me to Consciously Restart my life and how I found a new purpose, meaning and fulfilment. May this inspire *The Conscious You* from darkness to light.

My journey into a life I didn't choose, and certainly didn't want, began on a normal Thursday in October 2017. My husband, Chris, left for work, just the same as usual and I went on about my day. I was running a local Citizens Advice Bureau, working part-time and loved the work/life balance we'd created together. A usual day in the life of me, Carey, was letting Chris get up and organised, a quick chat about plans and what to have for dinner then he would head off for his day and I would get the hounds sorted, run any errands, get some housework done and then I would start work at eleven. I finished at four in the afternoon and had plenty of time to shop and organise our dinner before Chris came home. Our life was running smoothly, I loved our routine.

We had just had an amazing trip to the UK for a family wedding, a stopover in Dubai, and made some amazing memories. Plans were afoot for my upcoming fiftieth birthday, a truly special trip that we had dreamt of taking for some time. We were comfortable and happy with many exciting years ahead of us.

Then, in an instant, my whole world was turned upside down and there were never going to be days like I was used to again.

It started when I had a call from one of Chris' workmates. I had a funny feeling about it as he was asking to meet up with me, he sounded cagey, so I said I would leave work early and meet him at home. I was becoming more uneasy and tried calling him again, he said "*we're nearly there*", it wasn't until sometime later that I picked up on the "*we're*" part of what he said. I was on tenterhooks, looking out the window, when I saw him come to the front gate, I then noticed the two policemen standing behind him.

I knew the news wasn't going to be good, nothing could prepare me for the news they shared with me that day. Chris had died suddenly, at his workplace earlier that day. He had been found unresponsive and alone. I couldn't wrap my head around it; I knew it must have been true, there were police in my home, I couldn't understand it or process it.

How are you supposed to react to these things? I had no idea what I was meant to think or feel, I was awash with every emotion and I was drowning. Inconsolable, confused and terrified, I remember vaguely thinking '*I need Chris to help me make sense of this, he'll know what to do*'. I was instantly plunged into a world I knew nothing about, with no instruction manual and no tools to call upon.

When someone dies suddenly the police have to treat it as suspicious, which was chilling in itself. All of Chris's possessions were at the police station. They were asking questions about Chris and our life together, they wanted to speak to our GP, and they were subtly looking around our home.

Suddenly, the house began to fill with people, Victim Support, my closest friend, neighbours, so many people, all completely shocked. The evening passed in a blur, the police left, others came and went, and I was finally left with our two closest friends.

Already I'd had to make some choices, whether or not to visit Chris (which the Police advised against), would I oppose a post-mortem, what funeral director would I want to use? How on earth had I come to a place where I had to think about these things?

That day cast a shadow over my whole existence and my future.

My first visit with Chris was two days later at the funeral home. I remember it so clearly, saying to the funeral director, "*once I go through this door it all becomes real*". My heart was breaking, seeing the man I planned to grow old with, just lying there. Right at that moment I was lost, not capable of any clear thoughts, it was real.

It was a while later that I found out through the Coronial Service, that Chris had died of an embolism and that his passing would have been very quick. In some ways, I took comfort from this as I hated the thought of him suffering alone. Finally, there was an answer that I could accept.

In those very early days I relied on those around me to guide me. Writing lists, checking in on how I was doing, feeding me, even walking my hounds. During all of the organising and life admin that needed taking care of, the one person I would always have turned to, was missing.

I felt adrift from everything, I had no idea who I was, or what I was going to do, I questioned every action and thought, '*Am I behaving in a way that is expected of a widow?*' I tried many things, grief counselling, on-line forums but nothing seemed to work for me. I was going through the necessary motions, some days more successfully than others. I wasn't sure what I was expecting, to be honest, through these experiences. Some connection to others who understood or had got through a similar ordeal perhaps? I didn't know what I needed or how I was going to live again.

I never imagined that I would have to contemplate my life without Chris by my side to make the big decisions. It hadn't been that long ago that we had chosen to move to New Zealand from our home in the UK and create a new life for ourselves. We got the hounds, a beautiful home and made some amazing friends. We were set, happy and had a plan for where our life was going together.

I wasn't meant to be making decisions about who I was, and what I wanted, alone. I had a plan, we had a plan, and now it was all lost and meaningless without Chris.

I reached a watershed moment in March 2018. I was not coping, I would arrive at work in tears, I couldn't think straight, I had no idea of who I was or what I was going to do. I met up with Alison for a coffee and a catch up. We had connected a while back through her work with Mindfulness, supporting those who were suffering through anxiety from the Earthquakes in New Zealand. We had briefly had a few sessions previously to help me stop smoking and it had worked, until all this occurred. I still remember Chris being so proud of me for quitting and I wanted to make him proud again.

Alison and I had stayed in touch, and she knew about Chris'

passing. During coffee, we had a conversation that went a bit like this:

Alison: "*How are things going?*"

Me: "*Oh ok, going to work is good.*"

Alison: "*Why?*"

Me: "*Because everyone tells me it is good for me.*"

That "*why*" in our conversation was a lightbulb moment for me. I realised in that moment that '*them*', '*they*', '*everyone*', weren't on my journey. I was being led by what I was being told would be good for me. I wasn't even attempting to process what had happened for myself, I was doing what I was told was expected of me. I needed some control and direction to make sense of my new life, and that's exactly what I vowed to do.

Having always been a mentally proactive person I started working with Alison, though she questioned me hard on my intentions for Coaching through this process. I was adamant that having tried every other grief process going, I wanted to run this one my way. And so, we got started.

One of the first things we looked at were beliefs. What were mine, what were others, and what were societies. Actually, sitting down and writing and reflecting on this was such a revelation to me. I had always wanted to conform and be seen as a positive influence and member of society; I was polite and well mannered and compassionate. In this new brave world that I was entering I had a choice to start to believe and behave in a way that felt natural and true to me. Like I said before there was no manual to follow here or tools at my disposal. So, I began to create my own.

Taking a real look at yourself, how you think, react and interact with the world is tough. For me, I held Chris close in this process, I tried to see myself through his eyes. What were the things he liked and admired in me? How could I build on these to create a life that was fulfilling for me, but true to who I was and wanted to be?

I had been so miserable at work, I wasn't holding myself to the professional standards I once held in high regard, I couldn't. The wave of emotions would come and go without warning and to be honest seeing people walking on eggshells around me was also a constant reminder of what I was going through and how I was seen as fragile. I didn't believe that staying at work and having a routine was actually helping me at all.

Once I realised that work wasn't what I needed, despite everyone's advice, I was able to start inquiring within what it was, and my answer came loud and fast; it was purpose! I had to think about what gave me a feeling of satisfaction and happiness. This was something that I hadn't had to consider before Chris had gone, because I was so happy and satisfied with our life. It was like a whole new experience, and it felt hard navigating this newness, learning to know myself without Chris.

The bottom line, for me, was that volunteer work and being active in my community were incredibly high on the list of what gave me purpose, but that was looking too far ahead. I wasn't ready to give anything to anyone, what I needed right now was time to grieve, heal and think. I needed to spend some quality time reconnecting with myself, getting to know who I was without my soulmate, redefining my life on my terms.

I left my job, and felt immediate relief at having made that decision, and I set my sights on my personal development journey, a way to come to terms with my new unintended life, without Chris. A way to grieve for my lost love, a way to plan for a new future, one of my choosing and making.

This was the greatest gift I could have given myself.

Initially I was afraid of what others might think, would I become a hermit, or a sad widow who didn't leave the house anymore, what about depression? Thankfully I could talk myself through these worries sensibly, I had worked with Alison on reframing these concerns and I was now in charge. I knew what each of those scenarios would feel like to me and I made sure that every day I actively checked in to see if I were resembling these concerns. Thankfully I never did. The idea of being in control and making Chris proud of me in this new life drove me forwards. It still does.

Sometimes this was very hard, and I had lots of false starts, but I can say, today, *The Conscious Me* is consciously creating my new world and life. Some days it is a true leap of faith but by taking time to learn about who I am, and what matters to me, is helping me daily.

In the early months of grieving my sense of self was so diminished I felt sure that anyone looking at me could see '*widow*' tattooed on my forehead. Again, some focused conversation and reflection gave me a sense of perspective. I was putting my own assumptions out into the universe, and creating, for myself, negative feelings and anxiety in situations that hadn't occurred yet. Just looking at everything Leesa went through with her anxiety, I can appreciate a lot of her story from my own experiences, and I had never had anxiety before this.

I spent (*wasted*) a lot of time and energy on thinking about what others were thinking, '*was my house clean enough for visitors?' 'Did I look ok?'* I wanted to find a way to let these thoughts go, though honestly sometimes it was easier focusing on the external challenges than the internal ones. I knew the time would come where I would be empowered enough to be myself and accept myself without projecting my assumptions and wanting to fit in. That knowing, was a light at the end of a tunnel I was striving to reach.

I was comfortable in our home, and I certainly felt close to Chris here but everything around me started to feel too big. My first change was challenging. My kitchen furniture was something we had brought with us from the UK. It was large and reminded me that I was now eating alone. I took the plunge and arranged to have my large furniture taken away and to buy something new. The day my friends were coming to help I had to make a start on cleaning and moving things. This was incredibly painful and by the time they arrived I was in tears, but I knew I had to push through. This was me moving forward, making choices that worked for me, but I acknowledged my feelings and let myself grieve the change in my life. I was consciously choosing it, and I knew for me it was the right change and the right time, I was getting stronger.

When I was thinking about buying some new flooring for a room in the house that was looking tired (having two greyhounds leaves a lot of muddy paw prints) before I even looked in a shop I was having some internal dialogue that went a little like this,

'They will think I am a cheapskate if I don't want the most expensive product, I am hopeless with math's so I won't understand what they are talking about with measurements, do I want strangers coming into my home?'

I was so incredibly critical of myself and my capabilities back then, and worried what others thought of me so much, I am pleased to say now, how far I have come! In this instance though, what got me to go through with the interaction was identifying what I wanted and why, and setting some boundaries with the salesmen on the phone before I even went to the store. It was liberating to know what I wanted and why and be able to communicate it easily in advance. Now, I have boundaries for everything, and they support me so much (Beck was right when she spoke about boundaries being important!).

After getting my flooring samples to choose from I wanted to ask the opinion of someone else. But why? I had to really talk myself through the need for their opinion, I was used to making joint decisions not solo ones. I decided that they would not be the one living with the new flooring or paying for it. Making changes to my home needn't be for resale value, merely for my own enjoyment and pleasure. When I followed these thoughts to their end I was able to make the best decision for me, rationalise it and feel confident in it, but it took time. Making changes to your home after a loss is an emotional time but you have to remember it is still your home. After the flooring was completed in that room I created a space that reflected me, just some simple changes, a new chair, a painting and no TV.

Becoming a non-smoker was still a goal and during the last eighteen months I have both succeeded and regressed at times, but I know I can and will get there fully eventually. And I know Chris will be mighty proud of me, just as I will when it is time.

Alison and I discussed what were some things that I needed to experience, really challenge myself on, in order to live and create new reminders of how far I had come. I was basically creating a whole heap of new neural pathways in my brain, traversing life in a whole new way. I had no previous experiences to fall back on, that my brain could relate to in my life since Chris's passing and at times I felt like I was short circuiting. Thanks to this experiment to keep expanding and trying new things, as the new me, I have become a pro and am mastering my confidence triggers and responses to pretty much any adversity with ease. Now, every time I try something outside of my natural comfort zone I get such a feeling of accomplishment. Some of these things are bigger than others. Going to the cinema alone for the first time took a couple of attempts but I conquered my fear of being '*looked at*'. My first road trip with the hounds, staying in a town I didn't know was a milestone, I had faith and trusted myself and we had a good time.

At every stage I consciously chose how far to go with my experiments. Some days were easier than others, but I appreciated the magnitude of creation I was building for myself and I knew Chris was always in my thoughts, guiding me still and cheering me on. That was a comfort.

Early in my journey it became clear that words and the use of them was something that I found triggering. So along with looking at my beliefs I looked at the words and phrases I was using. I often said the phrase *"this might sound weird but.."* at the start of a sentence. Identifying this, taking time in my sessions with Alison to consider why I was saying this made me realise that this phrase diminished me and what I was about to say. I was making some assumptions about the person I was talking to and how they would perceive what I was going to say. This highlighted that I was not being true to myself. I consciously decided to stop and think when this phrase came to mind, I was becoming more self-aware, and I stopped saying it. To this day, I still do not say *"this might sound weird but..."* and I love that I could change that for myself!

I decided I needed some motivation and foundational words that reflected who I was and who I wanted to be, something to acknowledge my journey, my transformation, my guides and to anchor me. These words are still held very close to me, a talisman of sorts, and I was even gifted a beautiful canvas with them on, so I get to see them every day, they are *'Baby Steps', 'Kindness', 'Connection', Engagement' and 'Purpose'*.

Baby steps

Was chosen to remind me that it is ok to take time on my journey. Each day I could cope if I reminded myself that I didn't need to do it all right now. I still go back to these words if life and decisions start to overwhelm me. I break down whatever the difficulty or decision is, reflect on what I want to achieve and approach it piece by piece.

Kindness

When looking at my values and beliefs, what makes me tick, it is kindness. Being kind to myself and others each and every day. It is a word I would like people to use when describing me.

Connection

This word has many connotations but in the early days it was to remind myself to remain connected to the world.

Engagement

This is my action word. I use this to check in with myself on many levels, in the early days it was a simple as *"have I actually spoken to another person today?"*

Purpose

I identified that having purpose or serving a purpose was a motivator to me. As time has moved on my purpose has been more about sharing my experiences on the journey to help others.

I began reflecting on my days, often writing in my journal, linking everything back to these core words. I continue to live my life with these at the forefront of my mind as a blueprint to follow.

Life changing experiences come in many shapes and forms,

divorce, redundancy, illness and bereavement. They make us look at the world differently whether we want to or not. I still have days where I have to acknowledge how I am feeling about this life that I didn't choose or want, but I have tools to help me:

- I listen to what my mind and body is telling me and ask myself what I can do to help myself. This might be clearing my diary of non-essential tasks for a few days, taking some time for a walk somewhere that makes me happy, making time for coffee and a chat with friends.
- Connect with someone, share what I am feeling, be honest and vulnerable. This is a challenge as most of us are not really programmed to do this comfortably, but it can help us make sense of our jumbled thoughts.
- Take time to breathe and reflect on how far I have come. Re-read some of the things I have written.
- Celebrate my achievements and triumphs – however small.
- Choose to honour what or who you have lost in a way that is meaningful to you helps. A lot of the new things in my home have been purchased with Chris in mind, an acknowledgement of my grief journey, and my growing sense of self.

Nothing will diminish my love for Chris and the choices we made for our life together. Now I have a new life and a new way of thinking. By consciously choosing daily, weekly, monthly what is right for me is liberating.

I choose who to spend time with.

If I don't feel happy I tell someone.

I try new things.

I grieve and cry.

I get angry.

But, I keep going.

I reflect.

I understand myself, my emotions, my needs and wants.

Consciously restarting isn't something that happens to you. It is a choice that *The Conscious You* decides to make when you experience something, something that you do not want to define you, something that you do not want to be stunted by, and something that threatens your very existence.

Your life changing experience is just that, and you can consciously choose to restart it your way, or not. Honestly, either way it takes practise, it takes effort and perseverance. I am so grateful that I chose to take control, to invest in myself, my future and consciously choose to make the very best of it – and I hope that if you ever have to restart, that you can too.

As a guide here are the steps that I believe can begin to help you to Consciously Restart;

- **Choice** – *The Conscious You* has to actively choose that you want to restart, that you are committed to wanting to make a new life for yourself, in the best way possible.

- **Accept** – *The Conscious You* needs to acknowledge the change that has happened to you and understand that life as you expected is not going to be.
- **Be open** – *The Conscious You* hasn't been here before so be open to how you are feeling, what you are thinking
- **Write it down** – Write your thoughts, feelings and how your day has been. Ask yourself, honestly and kindly, if today has been a good day. Acknowledge what was good – become your own cheerleader.
- **Let go** – Don't dwell on the things that weren't so great, I like to think of each day as a lesson, not in terms of success or failure. If I learn more about me every day that can only be a good thing.
- **Try new things -** Experiment with the unknown, create new neural pathways in your brain and master any adversity like a pro! Allow it to be an accomplishment!

ABOUT CAREY BUCK

Carey Buck's world changed in October 2017. In a moment everything she believed her life was and would continue to be ceased to exist. Her husband had died, suddenly, at work, leaving her grieving for a life she had lost as well as her beloved husband.

In the aftermath of this devastating loss she has had to travel a path in life that she had not chosen, that she was not equipped for, and for which there was no instruction manual.

Now in her second year as a widow she has chosen to share her journey with others. She has created The Grief Room NZ where anyone on a journey of grief can share experiences, resources and thoughts. Carey is consciously shining a light on how to take control through the grieving process to live a fulfilled life, albeit a different one.

Carey is originally from the south of England, she moved to New Zealand in 2006, with Chris, to begin a new chapter in their life together. Living in New Zealand has brought both challenges and opportunities and it is where Carey has consciously chosen to call home and explore this new way of being.

E: careybuck.cb@gmail.com

B: https://theunexpectedwidownz.com/

facebook.com/griefroomNZ

“

THERE IS NO BETTER TIME TO BEGIN YOUR CONSCIOUS YOU CONNECTION THAN NOW, AFTER ALL THIS IS THE ONLY TRUE REALITY, YOUR PRESENT MOMENT

PUTTING THE CONSCIOUS YOU INTO PRACTISE

BY ALISON CALLAN

'If your past is memories, your future speculation, then surely this moment now is all that counts? Learn to be with it fully'.

This is the thought that springs to mind so often when I am with clients who are finally living the life they cast their vision for, not that long ago.

"I wish I hadn't waited".

I know this feeling. The strength of your inner voice in the moment that we are in when we have achieved everything we set out to, or more, which says *'wow, it wasn't as hard as I thought, I'm here, I wish I had done this sooner'.*

I love this internal dialogue because it signals a time where we need to reflect on our journey and appreciate the lessons that we have learnt, and how we have put those lessons into practise.

The act of reflecting often goes by unappreciated, yet I am a firm believer that we need to be especially conscious in this practise. Because if our present, and ultimately our future, is shaped by our past experiences, shouldn't we make sure that we are consciously present with the interpretation of them?

I was fortunate enough to experience another opportunity to change my life, to re-live a similar experience on the journey that started my exploration into Conscious Creation. This time though, I was connected to my Conscious You. Let me enlighten you further, and how I learnt to put *The Conscious You* into practise.

Max turned two in the summer of 2015, and I was pregnant. This time I didn't conform to waiting the usual twelve weeks, as I had with Max. I consciously chose to not keep our joy a secret, I was ecstatic from the outset and I wanted to share our news.

Being pregnant, plus managing a toddler, was a totally different story for me. The promise I had made when I was pregnant with Max, to enjoy every moment, in all honesty wasn't enough of an anchor this time in my connection to my consciousness. I wanted to explore that inner knowing, that I was meant to be doing something more in the world, that I could experience fulfilment outside of motherhood.

I didn't want to experience success only through the experiences of my children, and my motherhood journey. I had a life to live too, and I didn't want to miss a single second of it. The inner voice and connection to my purpose was getting stronger.

Our Liam arrived in September 2015, right on time and I was suddenly on parental leave again. This birth hadn't given me the kick of happy hormones that I had first time round. Yet we made it. And not long afterwards I felt the anxiety set in, just as Leesa described in her story.

I had no idea what I was doing with my life, outside of parenting, and where my success stories were going to come from. I did have one decision pretty firmly made though, there were no more children in my future I was done!

One night I found myself standing in the living room looking out again over the inlet towards the hills. It was 2am and I was rocking Liam to sleep, soaking up each second I had him in my arms. I began to think back over my journey.

The way I had chosen to navigate a brand-new, unknown path and how I had nearly succumbed to the negativity of everyone around me regarding the struggles of parenting, and if I had, would I have been there then, in that moment, actually enjoying my exhaustion with Liam? Probably not.

It was then in that moment, a mere two and a half years from the first time I had been standing looking out over those hills, contemplating my feelings and experiences, making my first conscious choice, that I could appreciate and really process the enormity of that realisation. How connecting to my consciousness had begun my journey to consciously choose my thoughts, feelings and beliefs, unlearning everything I was exposed to, about the common and likely parenting outcomes I would experience. Just like that, I knew the power of *The Conscious You*, how we decide what we believe, and what we let into our lives.

I was consciously creating my reality and breaking a mould I didn't know had existed within me before that moment.

The power of reflecting on my journey of learned and created experiences and choices enabled me to think bigger, to expand and determine what else I needed to break to rebuild, to unlearn to reprogram, to unleash and own.

I am now Consciously Creating my own success stories, the ones that I mentioned earlier, the ones that I was searching for, to give meaning and purpose to my life. And what's even better is that I'm also empowering others now to do the same.

You see, I knew it all along, it was always there, hidden behind my conditioning and learnt behaviour, behind my desire to fit in. Becoming the woman who knew I could do and be something more in the world, as well as be an incredible mother, was and is still a journey. I put my energy and intentions towards consciously creating my future, my story, my way. It only took thirty eight years, two pregnancies, a hell of a lot of sleepless nights and parenting challenges, internal battles, discomfort, a lot of changes in my beliefs and overcoming so many fears to get me there! And that was just the beginning!

The important part is I made it, and I am consciously owning it now.

And you can too.

I can be at peace with a lot of decisions that may not eventuate in the outcomes that I wished for, all because I am conscious with the decision-making process now and I define for myself a contract of sorts, that states, *'I am making this decision freely to the best of my abilities, in this moment with all the available knowledge that I have, and I am happy with this decision whatever the outcome that lies ahead'*.

I had to use this practise consciously a lot of times when deciding whether or not to travel to see my Mum when the boys were so young. It is still a challenging situation to be in, however I know that my conscious practise and contract with myself ensures I will never regret my choices and that I always do the best with what I have. Using this practise means that I do not have to go into reflection and come to terms with my decisions or experiences because I was fully present to the process. Utilising this allows me to focus in the present and be conscious of what I can do right now.

The difference in reflecting to learn and consciously create a new interpretation of an experience for my future, and reflecting to try and make sense of something in my present that I cannot process, is incredibly freeing. I am living with a lot more intention and purpose and taking responsibility for all that happens in my world.

This took me time to understand, and I have been connecting to my consciousness for quite some time now and putting it into practise, knowing that it is a lifelong journey.

Living as *The Conscious You* is not a gateway to enlightenment. I know it will expand your mind, lengthen out that 5%, allow you so much more joy, fulfilment and purpose, that does not mean that there won't still be challenges. You will just know how best to respond to those challenges, consciously with all of the tools that we have shared with you, at your disposal.

One of the biggest shifts that occurred in my life, and in all of the lives of my clients, is the actual practise of connecting to *The Conscious You* daily.

This is the practise which will get you thinking '*I wish I hadn't waited!*', which you now know is merely a trigger to have you appreciating and learning from the journey that you have been on. Everything you have experienced has brought you to this moment, exactly as it needed to.

Now, this is my very simple explanation of what I understand to be a complex system. Our subconscious works through the neural pathways in our brain which send signals to the body that then responds. Certain neural pathways in our brain have been used more frequently than others, and we can respond on autopilot.

Remember when you learnt to drive a car? In the beginning it took effort and concentration, however, there comes a time where you can be driving and your body is responsive, yet your mind wanders off and suddenly you notice you've arrived at your destination with very little memory of the experience. Your body knew what to do, what to look out for and where to go, somewhat automatically.

Our subconscious uses the neural pathways it is familiar with, so when we are rebuilding and programming our beliefs and choosing our responses, we need to concentrate on being in our *Conscious You* state, while we build new neural pathways for our subconscious to connect to. Therefore, overriding our original system preferences.

Remember all that Samantha shared with you in the power of Energetic Communication, and the states of language and intention for our subconscious mind to process? You must be intentional and clear about what you do want.

Putting *The Conscious You* into practise will take practice. It is not my intention to eliminate your subconscious mind, not at all. I want to bring to your awareness the areas in your life where you feel unfulfilled and show you that it is possible for you to connect to your Conscious You and Consciously Create your best life. Re-programming your subconscious mind by practising being in your conscious state to notice what isn't in alignment with your true desires, intentions and beliefs, will enable the neural pathways that you have consciously chosen to be the favoured ones by your subconscious. So that you develop habits and responses that uphold the vision and values that you have chosen to embrace for your life, as *The Conscious You*.

I have found that before we go to bed at night, and just as we wake in the morning are our best times to intentionally get into our Conscious You state. This is because we have usually finished our day or are just about to begin it, and both are optimal times for purposefully reflecting and reprogramming.

I created the Mindset Pathway[1] to support you in consciously creating your ultimate day, everyday. It is a practise I designed to consciously choose your preferred neural pathways, to become more emotionally intelligent and connect you to *The Conscious You*.

The purpose of this Pathway is to activate you in consciously creating and aligning *what* you are doing with *who* you are becoming while reminding yourself of your '*why*'. To ensure that each day is filled with meaning, momentum and a mindful Conscious You approach. Allowing you to consciously envisage, create and plan your personal pathway to success.

The Mindset Pathway has been developed to support you in retraining your brain into actively and consciously thinking about your day.

Imagine how much more meaningful your day would be when experienced through *The Conscious You*, through the choices you choose to make, and the actions you choose to take and how they extend to support your purpose. And how after practise and time your subconscious responds similarly with your preferred behaviours, habits and responses. Leading you towards living a fulfilled, purposeful and enjoyable life.

It is entirely possible, remembering that I said previously, *The Conscious You* requires energy, commitment, practice and purpose.

Using the daily mindfulness ritual and planning practises, you will invite into your life more clarity, emotional intelligence, resilience and reflection. Resulting in a deeper sense of self-awareness and over time, self-mastery.

There is a lot of emphasis in our lives on *doing*, however the Mindset Pathway is designed to bring you back to the fundamentals of *being The Conscious You*, as well as achieving. So that you associate your days with being in control, intentionally highly functioning, connected and productive. The Mindset Pathway gives you an amazing ritual in one daily routine to enable you to become consciously aware of the connection between your mind, body, emotions and sense of self.

An integral part of the Mindset Pathway is not only to make your intentions known for how you want to envisage and measure your success for *being* in the world. It is also to learn and consciously create enhanced habits and routines intentionally, which leads to clarity of purpose, understanding your personal success story while engaging *The Conscious You*.

This Pathway is a practice that you can adapt to take into account any one of the aspects of connection to *The Conscious You* that you want to prioritise working on to enhance. This could be improving a relationship, managing your anxiety, improved communication with the universe or a deeper appreciation of yourself and your purpose here. Whatever you choose to focus on, the practise of the Mindset Pathway can be the anchor for you to commit through working.

The morning ritual for the Mindset Pathway is to allow yourself time to consciously set up your day, your actions, your contribution in the world and to connect to this consciously. Remember I touched on this briefly connecting you to the feelings of success as a morning ritual? Well this is the Mindset Pathway in its entirety, to incorporate further attributes to expand your ritual.

The evening ritual for the Mindset Pathway follows your days intentions and reflects with compassion and curiosity enabling you to become self-aware. The ritual is designed to measure your learnings and development in a state of gratitude for all that you experienced.

I want you to enjoy these practices as part of your daily routine, while gaining valuable insights to support you towards living a life you love and deserve by actively engaging *The Conscious You!*

The Mindset Pathway Morning Ritual

This routine is designed for you to use every morning to get you engaging *The Conscious You*. To activate an intentionally focused mindset, ready to drive your day forward the way that you envisage it being, while supporting you into becoming the person you most want to be.

Follow the Mindset Pathway morning ritual to kick start your day by focusing on clarity of mind, awareness of your conscious, knowing your blocks and goals and creating your starting point, getting your head in the game for the day ahead! Use this tool daily as a morning mindfulness ritual, or throughout your day when you need to shift any residual heavy moods, energies or emotions that do not align with your outcomes.

For the best effects practise this ritual on waking, follow the steps laid out before you even get out of bed. After a while, the routine will become a way of purposefully living your life. You will become more emotionally intelligent, intentional and self-aware. With plenty of practise and a commitment to using this tool you will be able to focus on being in *The Conscious You* state at any point within your day.

Ask yourself these questions and journal or meditate to build your connection, it will take practise and consistency to see results;

'What's Alive in me?'

Notice what emotion is primarily present right now? How would you like to improve it, release it or up-level it? What would be a better and more productive feeling to create now? Tap into it.

'Breathe and Focus'

Take your time to breathe and be present with *The Conscious You*. Invest time in mental preparation to maximise your outcomes. Breathe, focus and you will *be* purposeful. Imagine your preferred emotion manifesting now in your body, prepping you for your day. Sit in gratitude for the magnificence that is life.

'What am I Bringing to today?'

You want to bring your best self to each and every day, moment by moment. Take the time to list the qualities you want to bring into your being and your day, keep them in mind as you progress through the moments. Make them an affirmation and show up for your day Consciously!

'Mindset Reset'

Check and notice your Mindset, be prepared to reset it when

necessary. Are you in a *fixed* or *growth* mindset? A fixed mindset is where you see and feel your limits and your language is focusing on the challenge. A growth mindset is where you expand to believe in your potential and solutionise an outcome. And about what specifically? This step can be replicated numerous times throughout your day!

- Notice your mindset.
- Recognise your ability to choose your mindset, either fixed or growth - own the decision.
- Talk back to your fixed mindset voice with a growth mindset response.
- Remember, '*I Can, I Will, I AM!*'

'What is todays Significant Goal?'

What must you achieve today? Set it up, name it, write it down and own it. If you're not sure, it's usually the lurking task and feeling of something you really don't want to do and know you must. So, commit here and now to get it done, using *The Conscious You* connection engage with the feelings you created, the qualities that you are bringing to your day along with your growth mindset, knowing that once you have achieved this goal the rest of your day can just *flow...*

'Motto - Today is...'.

Now you are tracking and firing on all the necessary levels to master your mindset and create the day you are envisaging, state it. Write a statement for today that resonates with your desired focus. Something to come back to, to keep you on track.

Maybe even use one of the quotes within this book that resonates and reminds you with ease to be with *The Conscious You*.

Evening Mindset Pathway Ritual

I have explained how powerful reflection can be as a practise to be in the conscious state learning with kindness and compassion. This is your mindful ritual for the evening to keep you in the present, aware of what you have learnt during the day you have just experienced, no regrets, pure direction and fuel for growth in our next day.

I recommend that you use this part of the process, the same time every day, usually after you've unwound from your work or business day, so maybe after your evening meal, or before your night time routine. This is your opportunity to record how you viewed your day in relation to living your ideal life. Notice where you aligned in thoughts, actions and behaviours, and where you didn't. See what comes up through this process for you and start to realise where your patterns lie.

Reflect on the following questions and either meditate, journal or discuss with a partner. Whatever your preferred method, get real, vulnerable and conscious!

'Reflection'

Check in on where you recalled *The Conscious You* and called into action your '*Moto*' and your '*Mindset Reset*', assess how this one special day fulfilled you, challenged you and where your areas of growth were.

'Gratitude'

This is your opportunity to incorporate the high vibe ritual of a gratitude rampage. This is literally where you get to write out, draw, tick off a list of all the things you are feeling grateful for from your day. As an activity, this will become easier as you practise, and it is designed to get you to see so much good in your day, even on the days that might challenge you. So, before you go to bed and close the day off, you know there was something magical about it.

I recommend that you write your rampage of gratitude out, then speak it aloud, allow yourself to say it all with as much emotion and feeling as possible, it's an incredible process and although it might feel uncomfortable to begin with, this will soon be the best part of your day, and something you look forward to.

'Align with your vision'

Everyday can contribute to your purpose, it either enhances the vision you have, amends it, or has you seeming or feeling off course. Committing to connect every evening with our thoughts, behaviours, language and actions from the day, determines and aids you to see how you may have moved further forward in your endeavours. So that you can keep connected to your '*why*', your development, your purpose and ground you with *The Conscious You*.

Please make sure that you don't beat yourself up at this point if you don't feel aligned or that you have moved forwards, this is the moment where you need to be truthful with yourself, all of yourself on your connection to your purpose and fulfilment and ensure it is what you actually want and need now, that it is supported by your belief systems, self-worth and mindset, otherwise you will be in some internal conflict. So, connect to *The Conscious You* get it out on paper now and ensure that your following days plans support your true vision.

Connecting to *The Conscious You* through using this Pathway or any of the suggestions in this book is only an invitation for you to become aware of what resonates, what feels expansive and possible for you now.

Later is a different story, and who knows how you will feel or what you will be ready to establish within your world.

There are no expectations only support and assistance, so if you need any help with any of the sections in this book when connecting to *The Conscious You*, then please reach out. We want to see you succeed in embracing the concept and putting it to use, to Consciously Create your best life!

“

IF THERE WERE NO OBSTACLES, FEAR OR JUDGEMENT, WHAT WOULD YOU WANT, WHO WOULD YOU BE, WHERE WOULD YOU BE?

WHEN THE CONSCIOUS YOU IS WORKING

BY ALISON CALLAN

'Success is a feeling'.

By now you are familiar with your conscious and subconscious mind, I know that you're learning a lot about yourself from even this first shift in your awareness and that's perfect.

This is a life long journey that you're on now and you have the benefit of leading the way through *The Conscious You*.

I know you're wondering, what do you do now?

I am hoping that by you being here you would have read Chapter two, Connecting to your Conscious, and have your list 'A', of where your life presently is, and list 'B' where you desire it to be. You may or may not have naturally uncovered some blocks or barriers that may be causing you some inner conflict in your pursuits getting from where you are now, to where you desire to be and believe it or not that there *is* progress.

You have absorbed so much information in this book, started to elicit your values and beliefs about the different aspects in your life and again how they might be supporting or creating resistance in getting you from your current list 'A' to your desired list 'B'. That's right, this is also progress.

You have been guided through my story and how I was able to catch my subconscious programming through my parenting journey. You heard how I consciously chose to recreate my values and beliefs at that time, and how the promise I made to myself, even before I knew what I was doing, became my anchor.

I shared with you my truths and insights that came up for me through my process of connecting to *The Conscious You* and how you could cause synergies or resistance in exploring your truths through them. How exciting, getting to tap into your underlying subconscious programs and beliefs!

I'm sure you're familiar with the feelings of success now, after our practises and morning rituals, how great does that feel? You know now that you can consciously create your feelings and elicit states of being whenever you need, it all starts with building your connection to your unique emotional intelligence. Knowing that you are not your emotions and allowing yourself to acknowledge all of the states you experience, how freeing.

Samantha shared with you the power of energetic communication and no doubt blew your mind in the process, so let's hope you're focusing now on more of what you desire and less of what you want to delete and reprogram. Use this genius method of Samantha's with those barriers and blocks you might have uncovered and see how your life experiences begin to expand.

And what about your relationships? Beck shared with you so many insights to have you take control and responsibility for choosing how to allow relationships into your life, and actively manage them and yourself to thrive, through boundaries, communication, emotional intelligence, curiosity and kindness. What useful and practical wisdom you now have to begin to transform your approach to those connections in your life, haven't you?

And you can practice some of those relationship goals with your surroundings too, combining Samantha's and Beck's wisdom as a foundation of learning into Jude's explanation of creating your soul space, how beautiful. Knowing how you too can communicate with the energy around you in your environment and the importance of its impact on you, fascinating!

If you know the feeling of anxiety then thanks to Leesa and her engaging story you can consciously develop control over this feeling, knowing the experience passes and you are always the winner, that's right. Remember *'I see you anxiety, and you will not win today!'*

Carey showed you her strength, courage and compassion for self. She highlighted her journey of consciously restarting and how utilising *The Conscious You* created a pathway she could build, empowered and aware, to create another life she loved, different but hers.

I shared examples of how putting *The Conscious You* can be used more in practice to build your connection and foundations, as well as taming the inner voice of '*I wish I had done this sooner*'. Now is the perfect time to get started, isn't it?

So why the combination of these topics, why these specific authors and journeys? I have worked with so many clients, and the connection that they all have is their drive to contribute more in the world, to follow their inner calling, that voice that says there is something more for them to be doing and being. Each time we connect and move them further along their path the foundational elements of their journeys require work in relationships, communication, removal of unwanted programs and subconscious beliefs. Then they connect to their space and surroundings and they restart as they mean to continue through *The Conscious You*. Each one of these authors who bring you their zone of genius in their chapters have passionately embraced their journey and evolved before my very eyes into the thought leaders they have become today. Able to share their exponential value around their passions and purpose with conviction and presence.

As you continue in your daily life you will experience nudges that bring *The Conscious You* to the surface. And you can feel it, the simmering curiosity, the trigger of newness in catching those thoughts, the diving for more information when you feel out of sorts, don't you?

This is how you will know that you are tapped in to *The*

Conscious You, it's a subtle shift during your day in your awareness. In the thoughtful planning you might make a touch more time to be present for, it's the creation of your Mindset Pathway, the improvement and fulfilment of more connection, time for yourself.

It is the awareness of barriers and blocks and it is the knowing feeling that you are meant to do more and be more in the world becoming a clearer vision that you want to embrace and explore on list 'B', without fear or judgement, because you're ready, aren't you?

There is no time limit or expire on this connection, it isn't something we master once and once only. *The Conscious You* is a progressive journey of evolution. Allow yourself to feel into one aspect a day that needs your conscious involvement, in order to create your best life and in a year, you will have made 365 shifts in your world which will present a whole new model of life to you.

We want this book to be one that you come back to and use time and time again as you uncover more about yourself, so you will uncover more depth here. What resonates today may be old news tomorrow. What you skim through today will be the missing link for the evolution of your awareness in the future.

You have everything you need to consciously create your desires, knowing this now, having the resources available to you in these pages for all time cements those foundations for you to grow, and you can allow it.

Be patient, be kind, be curious and be *The Conscious You*, now.

YOU HAVE, AND YOU KNOW IT ALL THAT YOU NEED. YOU ARE CONSCIOUS, RESOURCEFUL, AND INFINITELY WHOLE

BEFORE YOU GO

I would love to ask a favour or two of you, if you enjoyed this book please would you share this with your networks, friends and family, the more connected we all are to *The Conscious You* the better!

Connect with myself and each of these inspiring authors who have shared their genius with you in these pages for all time. You can see their links and contact details in their biography pages.

Post a picture of yourself on your social media with your copy of *The Conscious You*, be sure to tag me, and use the hashtag #TheConsciousYou, to get exclusive access to a very special bonus!

Share with us your shifts and how connecting to *The Conscious You* has supported you to expand and consciously create your best life, that's right, we want to celebrate your successes!

And of course, if you become a die-hard Conscious You fan, we would absolutely love a review on Amazon!

Thank you for allowing us to take you on the journey to becoming *The Conscious You*.

With immense gratitude,

Alison Callan

“

WHEN WILL YOU KNOW EVERYTHING?
NEVER, WE ARE ALWAYS EVOLVING.
SO, LEARN TO LOVE YOUR
JOURNEY CONSCIOUSLY

'THE CONSCIOUS YOU' QUICK REFERENCE GUIDE

THE CONSCIOUS AND SUBCONSCIOUS EXPLAINED

Knowing the difference for you, between your conscious and subconscious state is the beginning of tapping into your awareness, because in it's very essence consciousness is the state or quality of your awareness in any given moment.

Your conscious mind refers to those conscious experiences that you have where you are aware of your internal dialogue, your thoughts, experiences, feelings, memories and sensations in the moment.

The Conscious You is objective; it is your thinking mind and it is said that we are only in this conscious state for up to 5% of your day.

Your subconscious mind is the mental, emotional processor of activities just below the threshold of your consciousness, think of it like the hard drive of a computer, storing information and running programs. This hard drive contains mostly learned and absorbed behaviour, which is how we can function in the world and have our mind wander somewhere else entirely.

It is immensely powerful and controls the functions of our body, such as your breathing rate and heart beats. Our subconscious mind is in control of 95% of how we experience and show up in our lives.

When engaged *The Conscious You* can pick up on moments of thoughts and feelings and behaviours that arise subconsciously through the pre-programmed systems which store your beliefs, your habits, your responses and emotions.

The conscious mind, when aware and invested, can reprogram the subconscious to respond to life in our most favourable of ways.

* * *

THE CONSCIOUS YOU

Everything starts with us, our journey, our dreams, our wants, needs and environment. We can learn a lot about ourselves here and now, exactly where we are at. And this is exactly where we begin.

The Conscious You, is an invitation for you to connect with many of the aspects that you can actively work on right now to bring more fulfilment, joy and connection into your life.

It starts with evaluating where you are at now, letting that deep inner calling lead the way towards those long forgotten or dismissed dreams and connect to your conscious choices, actions and opportunities.

Life doesn't happen to you, it happens for you, and as such you need to take charge and begin to make changes in the moments where you can be present and conscious of your wants, needs and desires.

Becoming conscious enables you to get to a place where you feel deserving, worthy and ready to actively reach for your dreams and prioritise your happiness.

Everyone has a different version of what brings them happiness and what success feels like, rarely do we bring our conscious awareness to these aspects of us to prioritise them, allowing us to Consciously Create our best life. This is your opportunity – grab it!

* * *

CONNECTING TO THE CONSCIOUS YOU

Let's connect you to *The Conscious You* now by asking the following questions;

- Get familiar with your conscious mind, learn to recognise when it is naturally in control.
- Start to notice when your subconscious programs

come into play, and get curious about what that tells you.

- Write your list 'A' for what your life looks like presently, where are you, what do you do, how do you feel, what surrounds you and who are you spending your time with?
- Write your list 'B' for what you would prefer your life to look like? Where would you be, what would you do, how would you feel, what would be around you and who would you be spending your time with?
- Identify where in your life you're going through the motions.
- Focus on each answer and without too much thinking, allow your subconscious to respond to the questions;

◊ what do you know about what is holding you back?
◊ what do you feel about what is holding you back?
◊ what do you believe about what is holding you back?

- Notice any disconnects and similarities between all of these responses, what stands out to you?

I use this exercise often myself to determine what might be out of alignment in my life, and I invite you to do the same, with these lists I am sure you will see some synergies and disconnects.

Understanding how your conscious and subconscious mind works is the first step to unlocking your ability to be, do and have more of what you want in the world.

* * *

VALUES AND BELIEFS

Your values are a code by which you have chosen to live your life. Your values describe the importance of things, actions or behaviours which guide your attitudes towards or away from things. In a narrow sense your values are a moral compass of sorts, which, uniquely to you denote what is good, worthwhile or desirable in your world. These values drive your behaviours and they steer you towards or away from decisions, situations or behaviours.

Your belief is your truth, which is entirely unique to you based on your personal attitude, concepts and experiences. Beliefs are contextual and individual to each of us as they arise from our learned behaviours and our own experiences. These beliefs become your anchors to guide you through your life.

Now if we have values and beliefs, and these are created and stored over time as our programs to support us to better navigate this world through our subconscious in that thriving 95% of the time. Then anything that comes into our field of perception to challenge those values and beliefs is of equal importance. Because we also store programs around how we will respond and behave.

This is where you start to trust the unconscious mind because its primary role is to keep you safe and its programs have been created in order to do just that, to the best of its ability. Regardless of what arises trust that the intention until now has been for your good, now that you know more about the benefits of connecting to *The Conscious You*, you can do and be even better, if you choose to.

'Never allow your assumptions of how a situation might unfold to rule your experiences and expectations'.

- To re-write this for yourself and become the Conscious You;

◊ Begin to identify when you create assumptions, and consider how you would approach the situation differently if they were removed?
◊ Imagine a situation where this practice would have been of support to you.
◊ How can you recall it in future instances where it may be of support?

'When you consciously create your 'Why', you have purpose and intention'

- Here are some questions to ask yourself to help you in getting consciously connected to a more Conscious You;

◊ What is your '*Why*', personally and professionally? Are they aligned?

◊ What are the emotions connected to your '*Why*' ? How does it make you feel?
◊ Consider how knowing your '*Why*' will support you to successfully navigate all obstacles in your life.
◊ What can you do to remind yourself to recall and tap into your '*Why*' regularly?

'Your experiences can spark a passion that can be used to teach others and light a pathway to your purpose'.

- To begin to find your *Conscious You's* purpose and meaning in life so far, you can task yourself with these exercises;

◊ Make a list of your life experiences, note how you feel about them, how you journeyed through them and which ones you are most proud of.
◊ Journal the story and identify what you can teach others from your experience.
◊ Connect this to your '*Why*' insights, and you will begin to uncover your present purpose.

'Don't waste time and energy on an imagined future, especially if it makes you feel powerless and out of control'.

- To activate your more conscious mind in these situations, be sure to;

◊ Be self-aware.
◊ Be mindful of the time, energy and focus you give to thoughts which lead you astray and make you feel powerless and out of control. Therefore, identify those emotions and triggers.
◊ Instead stay in the moment and find your peace there.
◊ Concentrate on feeling more successful, assertive, and confident when you consider your future.

• Allowing yourself to trust that you are consciously creating your most empowered and connected version of your future in alignment with your '*Why*', knowing that all your assumptions and judgements are not needed, makes for a pretty powerful and Conscious You.

'Get Perspective'.

- Here are some ways that you can ensure your connection to your perspective, incorporating some of the other insights into *The Conscious You*:

◊ Connect to what brings you perspective.
◊ Where would perspective be most useful for you in your life right now?
◊ Create a morning mindset ritual to consciously connect to your '*Why*', your vision for your future, so you begin your day with the perspective that is going to ensure you make the most of it and attribute your actions and responses to life through this lens. So that

you consciously bring your best self to your day, every day.

- Gaining perspective like this allows us to remember our place in the world, to be a part of something bigger, greater and to be grateful for the experiences, always looking for the meaning.

'When stuck in the unknown, request that the Universe provide an answer, then listen'.

- When you need to offer up a situation for universal support ensure that you do so from a conscious space, so that you are actively open to receiving the response when it is presented. Here is how you can ask for this guidance for yourself:

◊ Ask a specific question before your dream state or during meditation.
◊ Once you have been clear in your question, make it specific then intentionally let the desire for an answer go.
◊ Let go of your preference to have a particular answer delivered. Be open to the options, they may pleasantly surprise you.
◊ Imagine detaching from the need for an outcome, knowing that it's already on its way.
◊ Consciously continue in your days with the resolu-

tion that an answer will be presented in the perfect time.
◊ Be patient!

- Remember that sometimes we only see the answers to our questions in reflection, not everything can be seen, experienced and appreciated during the occurrence. There is a reason that hindsight is universally known as a wonderful gift!

'It is more important what I think of myself, than what others think of me!'

- Well, here is the practise that you can use to tap into this insight;

◊ Notice when you are contemplating an outcome based on your assumptions of other people's perceptions.
◊ Enquire with yourself as to whether this is actually your internal fear, worry or belief.
◊ Remember that what you think of yourself is of critical importance and that this inner work always needs addressing.
◊ Turn your compassion inwards, be kind and curious towards your responses without attaching other people to your journey.

* * *

CONSCIOUS AND ENERGETIC COMMUNICATION

Awareness - Everything is energy and you are communicating all the time. Remember that your subconscious mind is automatically running your programs in the background. Regardless of whether the program is good, bad or detrimental, it's running.

Understanding - Your subconscious mind is creating most of your current reality. Your subconscious programs are constantly energetically communicating with your energetic force field, and the energetic force field is constantly looking for situations and circumstances to deliver on what you are communicating.

Commitment - This is the commitment you make to taking daily conscious action to fine tune *your* Energetic Communications and the reprogramming of your subconscious mind.

Deletion - This is the stage where you actively participate in changing your energetic communication through *The Conscious You* so that your subconscious can start to download updated programs, intentional programs that work for you. Take yourself through the process of deleting old programs, as in chapter 3.

New Programs - This is the most powerful way you can consciously create your best life. This is where you create a possibility of what your new programming could be. Take a list of possibilities and get into a conscious state. Give thanks and express gratitude for already experiencing these possibilities as actual realities in your current life.

Conscious Connections

Relationships are a choice. There are no relationships in your life that are forced upon you that you need to keep. It might feel that way sometimes, but it is not the truth. Not family, work, friends or partners are there forever, unless you choose it to be that way.

There are seven aspects that impact and influence your relationships;

- **Communication** – Remember to think before you speak, not everything that is in your head needs to be said, listen and tone.
- **Emotional Intelligence** – Tap into this through journaling, building your awareness. Remembering to breathe and being conscious of your physical reactions.
- **Boundaries** – This is your way of saying to someone, this is where I begin and end.
- **It's Not About You** – Remember to start with Compassion, be conscious of your triggers and tap into your empathy.
- **Masculine and Feminine -** Let it go, use your intuition, slow down and practise being present, get creative.
- **Respect** - Value both yours and the other persons needs and feelings, compromise, consciously create

boundaries, speak kindly, treat the other person as whole, practice self-respect.

- **All Emotions are Valid** - Learn to sit with all of your emotions, learn to sit with others in their emotions, when someone is going through any type of emotional experience validate their feelings.

* * *

THE RELATIONSHIP SELF-CHECK IN

Questions designed for you to reflect on the relationships in your life and assess their status, so that you maintain alignment with all the aspects that it takes for your consciously created, thriving relationships.

- Are you aware of when you are in your masculine or feminine state?
- When you spend time with people in the relationships you have chosen, do you feel energised?
- When you spend time with people in the relationships you have chosen, do you feel drained?
- Do you feel understood by the people around you?
- Do you feel fully able to be yourself around others?
- Do you know your boundaries in your relationships?
- Do you feel that you are able to communicate your boundaries with others?
- Do you feel that these boundaries get respected?

- Do you feel that you are able to identify, manage and express your emotions effectively?
- Are you able to actively listen to others without thinking about what you will say next?
- Are you able to sit in the moment and be present with yourself?
- Do you feel heard by others?

CONSCIOUS SOUL SPACE

You are not only in a relationship with people, but with your energy and your environment, so make the impact that you want. Here are the steps to Consciously Create your soul space.

Choose your space - Consciously choose your space, to begin:

- start with a small space
- start with a space you see every day
- start with a space you have complete creative control over

Assess your space - Grab your notebook and sit in or beside your chosen space. Answer these questions:

- What works for you in the space as it is?
- What isn't working for you?

- What do you love about this space?
- What do you need to use this space for?
- How does this space really feel to you?

Chat with your space - Sit in or beside your space and ask it what it wants. Write down any ideas or thoughts that arise, no matter what they might be. Ask your space how you can work together to create this. Allow this information to come through you, receive everything with kindness and curiosity, release all judgements and connection to a particular outcome.

Set your intention - Drawing on your notes, write a list of words that describe how you want this space to be and feel. Review until you have a list of two to five keywords for your space. These are your intentions for this space. Make these into a sentence: "*My (space) feels ____, ____ and _____*".

Clearing and cleaning - Clear everything out and off your space, and clean the space thoroughly. I recommend cleaning/dusting everything as you take it out. Find a safe place to put things, even if it's just alongside. Yes, it will look messier for a bit. That's okay, it's only temporary.

Create and curate - Now you get to put things back in!!

Dedicate and enjoy - Deeply connect with your freshly souled space and enjoy it. To dedicate your space, do one or more of these (adjusting to suit your space):

- light a candle in your space and watch it burn, feeling the energy charge the space.

- breathe deeply and slowly, letting the air from your lungs fill the space.
- hold a cup of water in your hands and send loving energy to it, flick this water around the space or sit in the space and sip the water slowly.
- place your hands palm down on the surface of your space, close your eyes and feel the texture of the surface, feel where your hands meet the space, feel the energy that flows between you and your space.
- Sit in your space and enjoy it. Use it as you intended.
- Jot down in your notebooks your impressions of your space now.

* * *

CONSCIOUSLY CONTROLLING ANXIETY

If you have anxiety, you are not weird. It's just that your flight and fight responses are extreme. Everybody has this, yours is just a little off the usual charts, which makes you special!

When overwhelm and anxiety creep in, here are the tools to help you manage and create your best life. Remember with each anxiety attack it will build your resilience and courage. By staying one step ahead of your anxiety you become prepared, ready to fight.

- See your doctor.
- Do you need medication or perhaps a natural supplement?

- Do you need extra help, counsellors, psychiatrists, naturopaths, acupuncture etc.? (don't be afraid to get help, you deserve it!)
- Grab your own cheerleaders, those who understand and are there for you 100%!
- Take baby steps to gain control of your life. Gently push yourself to try, maybe that means driving yourself to the destination having a little bit of control makes you more eager and confident.
- Distract yourself, don't let anxiety win.
- As time goes by, push yourself harder and further don't miss out on life at least try, after all what's the worst thing that can happen? Anxiety will occur at some point, and will anyone even notice?
- Make yourself comfortable surround yourself with familiarities. Sit outside at a restaurant where it's cooler and not so crowded, grab a theatre seat at the end of the aisle, map out your exit strategy (it's ok, you probably won't use it) your thoughts are comforted and gives you thc courage to go further.
- Exercise to your liking, Meditation, yoga etc.
- Sleep well!
- Watch your own limits and take time out.
- Say "*No*".
- Eat well, does coffee or alcohol make you more anxious?
- Celebrate your wins!
- The most important, talk about it
- Laugh!

* * *

CONSCIOUSLY RESTARTING

Here are the steps that you can use to begin to help you to Consciously Restart;

- **Choice** – *The Conscious You* has to actively choose that you want to restart, that you are committed to wanting to make a new life for yourself, in the best way possible.
- **Accept** – *The Conscious You* needs to acknowledge the change that has happened to you and understand that life as you expected is not going to be.
- **Be open** – *The Conscious You* hasn't been here before so be open to how you are feeling, what you are thinking
- **Write it down** – Write your thoughts, feelings and how your day has been. Ask yourself, honestly and kindly, if today has been a good day. Acknowledge what was good – become your own cheerleader.
- **Let go** – Don't dwell on the things that weren't so great, I like to think of each day as a lesson, not in terms of success or failure. If I learn more about me every day that can only be a good thing.
- **Try new things -** Experiment with the unknown, create new neural pathways in your brain and master any adversity like a pro! Allow it to be an accomplishment!

* * *

PUTTING THE CONSCIOUS YOU INTO PRACTISE

I created the Mindset Pathway to support you in consciously creating your ultimate day, everyday. It is a practise I designed to consciously choose your preferred neural pathways, to become more emotionally intelligent and connect you to *The Conscious You*. The purpose of this Pathway is to activate you in consciously creating and aligning *what* you are doing with *who* you are becoming while reminding yourself of your '*why*'. To ensure that each day is filled with meaning, momentum and a Conscious You approach. Allowing you to consciously envisage, create and plan your personal Pathway to success.

The Mindset Pathway Morning Ritual

- 'What's Alive in me?'
- 'Breathe and Focus'
- 'What am I Bringing to today?'
- 'Mindset Reset'
- 'What is todays Significant Goal?'
- 'Motto - Today is...'.

Evening Mindset Pathway Ritual

- Reflection
- Gratitude
- Align with your vision

“

PRACTICE CREATES A PERMANENCE!

— Alison Callan —

COMMUNITIES

The Conscious Creation Community – Alison Callan

https://www.facebook.com/groups/ConsciousCreationers/

The Copywriting Coach – Samantha Haddad

https://www.facebook.com/groups/soulfulcommunications/

All things Love – Beck Thompson

https://www.facebook.com/groups/213078846124284/

Empowered Land Healing – Jude Smith

https://www.facebook.com/groups/311160796130670/

The Anxious Entrepreneurs – Leesa Watt

https://www.facebook.com/groups/theanxiousentrepreneurs/

The Grief Room NZ – Carey Buck

https://www.facebook.com/groups/1976309022673843/

“

ONCE CONNECTED YOU CAN NEVER GO BACK, BECAUSE WHEN YOU KNOW MORE, YOU CAN BE MORE

NOTES

2. CONNECTING TO YOUR CONSCIOUS

1. *'The Honeymoon Effect'* by Dr. Bruce Lipton, 2014 – references to the time spent in the conscious and subconscious states (95% subconscious and 5% conscious mind)

6. CONSCIOUS AND ENERGETIC COMMUNICATION

1. Morris Massey - The Massey Developmental Stages
2. *'The Secret'* by Rhonda Byrne, 2006
3. Gaia TV - www.gaia.com
4. *'Missing Links'* by Gregg Braden, 2017

8. CONSCIOUS SOUL SPACE

1. 'KonMari'd' – Marie Kondo
2. 'clutterbusted' – Clutter Busting with Brooks Palmer
3. 'S.H.E.D' – 'Shed your stuff, change your life' by Julie Morgenstern, 2009
4. 'feng shuied' – originates from ancient china, using energy sources to harmonise individuals with surrounding environments.
5. A whare nui is a beautifully decorated Maori 'meeting house' filled with carvings that represent and embody the ancestors of that tribe.
6. Note for more youthful readers: web rings were a way of linking websites on similar topics so you could jump between sites without having to reload your Altavista search. This was in the dark days before browser tabs and Google.
7. *'The Artist's Way'* by Julia Cameron, 1992

9. CONSCIOUSLY CONTROLLING ANXIETY

1. 'One Flew Over the Cuckoo's Nest' by Ken Kesey, 1962

11. PUTTING THE CONSCIOUS YOU INTO PRACTISE

1. The Mindset Pathway, by Alison Callan (http://bit.ly/MsPaP)

Made in the USA
Middletown, DE
25 June 2024

56246969R00151